The DEATH of SEO

An Internet Millionaire's How-to Guide to SEO Success

Charles Bosse

The DEATH of SEO

National Library of Australia Cataloguing-in-Publication entry (pbk)

Author:	Bosse, Charles, author
Title:	The death of SEO : An Internet Millionaire's How-to Guide to SEO Success / Charles Bosse
ISBN:	9780994374516 (paperback)
Subjects:	Internet marketing. Web search engines. Web sites--Registration with search engines. Web sites--Design. Web site development. Success in business.
Dewey Number:	658.872

Published by Charles Bosse and InHouse Publishing
www.inhousepublishing.com.au

Printed using Envirocare paper

Legal Disclaimer

Limit of Liability/Disclaimer of Warranty: While the publisher and author have used their best efforts in preparing this book, they make no representation or warranties regarding the accuracy or completeness of the contents of this book. The publisher and author specifically disclaim any implied warranties of merchantability or fitness for a particular purpose, and make no guarantees whatsoever that you will achieve any particular result. Any case studies or insights that are presented herein do not necessarily represent what you should expect to achieve, since business success depends on a variety of factors. We believe all case studies and results presented herein are true and accurate, but we have not audited the results. The advice and strategies contained in this book may not even be suitable for your situation, and you should consult your own advisors as appropriate. The publisher and the author shall not be liable for any loss of profit or any other commercial damages, including but not limited to special, incidental, consequential, or other damages. The fact that an organisation or website is referred to in this work as a citation and/or a potential source of information does not mean that the publisher or author endorses the information the organisation or website may provide or the recommendations it may make. Furthermore, readers should be aware that internet websites listed in this work may have changed or disappeared after this work was written.

Earnings Disclaimer: We don't believe in get-rich-quick programs—all human progress and accomplishment takes hard work. As stipulated by law, we cannot and do not make any guarantees about your ability to earn any money with our ideas, information, tools, or strategies. After all, it takes hard work to succeed in any type of business. In fact, it takes hard to succeed at ANYTHING in life—try learning to play the guitar without putting in any work, and see how that goes! Your results in life are up to you and the amount of effort and resources that you are willing to put into succeeding. Nothing in this book or any of our websites is a promise or guarantee of results or future earnings, and we do not offer any legal, medical, tax, or other professional advice. Any financial numbers referenced here, or on any our websites, are simply estimates or projections, and should not be considered exact, actual, or as a promise of potential earnings—all numbers are illustrative only. In fact, the average person who purchases this book and other programs never finishes the book, never puts the work into implementing the strategies taught, and therefore achieves little to no results. Thank you for reading.

www.thedeathofseo.com

Contents

Foreword

As small business owners, we have always needed to wear many hats—manager, accountant, salesperson, customer service rep, strategist, the list goes on and on—and the move to online marketing has just added to our daily to-do lists. We know that SEO is something we must focus on to ensure the very survival of our businesses, but it often falls by the wayside; not enough hours in the day, not enough money to allocate, not enough knowledge to achieve real results. But here's the fantastic part—you don't need to learn it all, to do it all. You don't need to master the technicalities of algorithms, metrics, and the like.

The best advice is to engage an SEO professional or team to help you. So why would you need this book then? Well, if you are going to outsource the reputation, the traffic generation, the connections with your target audience, and the online sales of your business, then I wholeheartedly suggest you have an understanding of the basics. You must understand 'white hat' and 'black hat' techniques; how recent changes have affected SEO; and the future of SEO, in order to select the right SEO professionals to work with and ensure that they are doing the right thing by your business.

Charles has created, with this book, a go-to guide that will explain, in easy-to-understand terms, the importance of SEO in today's market and how to implement the right tactics in your business. This is a rare opportunity to learn from someone who has already 'been there and done that' and now makes millions every year online.

Regardless of your industry or type of business, this book will help you understand how to achieve online success.

Connie Baker
Owner of Integrated Copy
Content & social media marketing consultant

Introduction

Is SEO dead? Over the past few years there has been plenty of conjecture about the relevance of Search Engine Optimisation or SEO and whether or not some of the recent Google updates have all but destroyed SEO tactics. It's a very important question you will need to answer if you own a website and/or want to earn an income from it.

This book will answer that question for you, in detail, and by the end of this you will know what you need to do to succeed online in 2016. If you want your visitors to actually find your website then doing nothing, or letting nature take its course will not work; you're doomed to fail.

I have made, and still make, millions of dollars from my websites in various niches and I can assure you that the websites I don't do any SEO on will stay firmly ranked halfway down the 7th page of Google. Maybe your website is there right now.

Over the past ten years I have spent a ridiculous amount of money and energy figuring out the best way to get my websites to generate income. I do not pretend to be the world's leading expert on SEO, I'm sure there are some very talented people out there in this space. Unfortunately the bulk of the industry is happy to take your money and deliver very little, which is why some basic knowledge as a business owner is key. If I had not had such bad experiences I don't think I would have ever been forced into learning this stuff for myself.

Over the past five years especially, I have learned the very best SEO strategies that have returned millions of dollars to me. This book will save you years of your life and plenty of wasted money as well.

This book is by no means exhaustive, and it's not a comprehensive overview of everything you can do online to drive traffic to your site. In fact, this book is the opposite; it's the 101 basics of SEO to survive online in 2016. As a website owner you can get hung up on all the hundreds of things you could be doing to make your website better, but this will keep you stressed and poor. Just focus on the basics. This book covers those basics.

At the end of this book you will at least know enough to direct your SEO efforts, if you are not going to do it yourself. You need to use this as a guide to make sure you are spending money on the right things.

I don't think the average business owner has time to keep up with or do all the SEO needed on a site. I think you should outsource it so you can focus on what makes you money: your core business operations. That said, you do need to have an understanding of what it takes to succeed online.

I hope you get something truly valuable from this book. Enjoy.

Charles Bosse
The Death of SEO
www.thedeathofseo.com

Section I
SEO Success

Chapter 1—The Demise of SEO

Meet Bob and Sue. About one year ago Bob and Sue decided to buy a health retreat in the mountains, looking for a change and an opportunity to have their own business. Sue is an experienced beauty therapist and personal trainer; Bob has a background in finance. They sold their house in the city and borrowed about as much as they dared and bought the business. Along with Bob and Sue the retreat employs about twenty staff and is doing ok, but the greatest challenge is getting their message out there. Between them they don't have any experience in sales or marketing and all they know about a website is that the previous owners have built one and it looks pretty good, with lots of nice pictures. Bob knows from the numbers that if they don't do something about getting new visitors to the retreat soon the business will die. Bob and Sue want to get their website working for them at the moment because at the moment they rely solely on word-of-mouth. When they searched health retreats in their area their site was nowhere to be found.

They wondered how to be found on Google. Bob has been spending considerable time trying to find out what exactly he should do for the retreat's website to be found. They have recently learned that to get traffic they need a good Search Engine Optimisation (SEO) strategy. They thought that shouldn't be too hard.

They soon learned that there are plenty of online marketers preaching a very interesting doctrine, a doomsday doctrine in fact, espousing the death of SEO or Search Engine Optimisation. In other words all the work you do to your website on-page or off-page no longer counts for anything, because Google is too smart. Essentially when it comes to this particular subject, everyone seems to offer up a different opinion. No one seems to know the facts and yet plenty of experts are willing to offer up a cure-all.

Recently the Slingshot Institute (www.slingshotinstitute.com) conducted the world's largest and most comprehensive SEO study. What this mammoth study demonstrated, in black and white, is that SEO is not dead, or dying for that matter. Where the uniformed in the industry are wrong, is that in reality SEO is not dead; it's just changing. So don't panic if you're a newbie like Bob or Sue to the field of SEO. Like them, you've probably been inundated with conflicting messages. We understand and this book is here to set the record straight for you.

'The days of SEO being a game outsmarting algorithms are over. Today content strategy and valuable, sustainable strategies are essential, not just tricks and links.'

Adam Audette
Chief Knowledge Officer, RKG

On one hand, you have been told that SEO is the only way to have website visibility and that this online presence helps you connect with new customers and rank well in search engine results. On the other hand you have been exposed to the fear of SEO's 'black magic', hearing that it is ineffective, outdated, and ruled by spammers. You have heard that there are 'black hat' and 'white hat' schemes and that the only way to succeed is to bad-mouth or destroy your competition. So how in the world can you be expected to know what to actually think about SEO?

Just a little bit about me: I make millions of dollars every year online and only online. Getting ranked number one in Google is my passion, but more importantly, making money online is the key here. There is absolutely no point in having a website about the green tree frog found under Mrs Smith's kitchen sink last December if it doesn't make you any money. Anyone can get ranked with that particular interest, however making a profit from that website is something entirely different.

Google is constantly changing. Are you?

The fact that SEO and/or Google, Bing, or Yahoo is moving the goal posts almost daily is absolutely no problem if you know what their endgame is.

While in the past SEO referred to a series of strategic approaches that you would take to make your site number one on search engines like Google, Yahoo, and Bing, its role has become more complex as the way that people search has become more complex.

If you were to have looked at an SEO plan in the past, it would have been a fairly straightforward process. You would have been offered advice and strategies on how to build links, structure a website, select the ideal domain name, and centre your content on the core principle you wish to promote.

In 2016 however, a professional SEO company needs to be all this and more. To be a beacon in the complex sea that is the digital ocean, you need to have logical and clear-cut tactics working for you. To compete successfully you need an SEO campaign that aims to balance the elements of links, content, and keywords. This includes, but is not limited to, unique content that draws interest, quality, and trusted links, an active social media presence, and above all a clear understanding of your target audience and what they wish to see. They should not only find your site, but want to engage with it.

What does SEO mean for me in 2016?

In 2016 SEO focuses on a principle of integration. This process brings together multiple disciplines: keyword research, search optimisation tactics, national marketing, local marketing, social media presence, copywriting, content development, and more.

To use a simple analogy, it's a bit like this: years ago all you had to do to have a great picnic in the Google park was turn up with a blanket (backlinks) and you could have a great time getting high rankings and being Mr or Mrs Popularity. However, Google got tired of these wannabe picnickers not really being committed to having a good picnic, just pretending to, so they came up with a strategy. They started requiring that you not only bring your blanket (still very important for any picnic, by the way) but you also need to bring chairs, food, cutlery, something to drink, and a few friends. If you don't turn up with these picnic items, then you're not really having a picnic, are you? You're not really committed to having a great time and ensuring everyone else does too.

This means that if you intend to have a website rank well in the world, your business needs to take heed of the wide scope of the current SEO universe. You cannot simply go at it alone, there are no more quick fixes, and no more underhanded schemes. You cannot simply think that you can tackle one area only, or do an average job in all areas; you need to place a high importance on as many SEO disciplines as possible.

At the end of the day, the intention of a search engine is to display the best result, so if you have put the time and effort into your website quality then you are clearly better equipped and more deserving of the business being sent your way. Overall, modern SEO has pushed the process back into the daylight so that dubious tactics will no longer be successful; it is more merit-based, and if you invest in effective SEO it will pay off for you.

Organic Search

To put it all in perspective for you; in 2016 we are rapidly approaching one billion websites (1,000,000,000) and every second of every day there are approximately 48,950 Google searches—and that figure is growing. These websites exist on any number of topics, and your business will want to be number one every time a relevant search is made.

In order for Internet users to negotiate this sheer volume of information, we use search engines. The ultimate goal of a search engine is to provide a searcher with a positive customer experience by providing the ideal result for their parameters. This means that the aim is to provide a helpful, high quality website that is known to be reliable and that will deliver the best result according to what a user wanted when they began their search.

Keywords are power. When it comes to a search engine, it is the keywords that are used to link the search parameters to the results and therefore the websites they display. They are the basis upon which the whole system of search engines works. But, as you can imagine, when you consider one billion websites, it can hardly be sufficient to simply ask, "Does the site contain the keyword searched for?" The result would most likely be ten million irrelevant websites and the internet would cease to function or provide any real, usable value. It is for this reason that Google and other search engines have developed algorithms to create a sophisticated, complex, and accurate means of not only distilling websites down to keywords and elements, but sorting what results should be at the top of the list presented to the searcher.

The exact algorithms that Search Engines use are a closely guarded secret, and updates constantly change the way that the algorithm functions, but it is simple enough to deduce the core principles and act accordingly. Some of these include the way in which a website is structured, the number and quality of links, what the content is and how well it is respected, and the way keywords are implemented.

Because of the changing nature of this field, it is challenging to maintain a complete understanding of how the algorithms are changing and being implemented. Your best hope is often an SEO specialist business that will have not only a current understanding of how best to optimise your website, but would have had to adapt in the past, will be required to stay abreast of any changes, and therefore can prepare you for what may happen next.

Website Traffic

There are all different forms of traffic that may engage with your website, and it is important to focus your efforts not just in one area, but to encourage all manner of ways for people to stumble upon your digital endeavours. To give an indication for the types of traffic you should consider:

- Organic/natural traffic—your typical search engine results as displayed through Google, Yahoo, Bing, etc.
- Social media traffic—the traffic encouraged or linked through your participation and presence on sites such as Facebook and Twitter.
- Paid traffic—the traffic that is a result of advertising campaigns such as PPC (pay per click), banner ads, or programs such as Google AdWords.
- Referral traffic—when links from other websites send visitors to you.
- Direct traffic—this is where your URL is typed directly into the browser.

Because SEO has broadened so much by necessity, while it may have simply been organic traffic a few years ago, a successful SEO campaign will now encompass and target all forms of traffic. You must always keep in mind that SEO in 2016 is about striking a balance between optimising for a specific need and diversifying to protect yourself against changing trends. This means broadening your horizons to new approaches that you may never have considered before.

The SEO Competition

What Bob and Sue quickly realised is that at all times in SEO you are in direct competition with every other website in your field. Each one is vying for the coveted first place in search engine results. This is why it is important to explore and consider your competition when devising an SEO strategy. It is often a misunderstood concept, because while there are limited spots on the first page, first place isn't everything. A 2013 study shows that first position on Google receives 32.5% of the clicks, the second position 17.6, and the third position 11.4. So this shows that yes, a higher position correlates to more traffic, but there is still a level of competition between all players. Competition is not a straight-forward process; it is infinitely more complex than it was even a few years ago. Don't be put off by the process; there is no overarching monopoly over the search results.

Thanks to the changes that have been made in recent years, the whole process is more merit-based than ever. If you are a growing business delivering real results, then with a professional SEO strategy you don't need to fear rivalry.

1st Page Search Statistics in Google

Why does SEO keep changing?

One of the most common questions asked is, "Why are there so many changes?" and, "Why do search engines keep making it harder for businesses?" The truth is that this isn't the aim of the search engine process. The intention isn't to make it harder, but to make it fairer, more accurate, and more user-friendly. The role of the search engine is to create the best possible experience by delivering the ideal results to a searcher. They don't intend to deny you access; they want to provide a clear road to the websites that offer the best content. It is a process of constantly raising the bar to encourage a general improvement in content so that everyone is happy.

The other reason for the changes is to continue to encourage the right practices in SEO. Forever plagued with a shady history, the SEO process has been dragged out of the shadows and away from dodgy and artificial practices. The attack the Search Engines have launched against the spammers and 'black hat' practices has resulted in the essential demand for quality sites delivering quality content in ethical ways. This may seem like it is more work for those at the ground floor trying to construct the perfect site, but the end result is that from the very start new content is being created on a sturdy foundation. By having a professional SEO service engaged in the generation of your site, to the perfect SEO standards demanded by today's society, you will not only be benefiting your site but also giving the best recognition to your brand and company in the long-term.

If Bob and Sue have the only health retreat in the small town they are in then ideally Google wants their retreat to come up at the top of the results because it provides the most accurate result. To have a retreat listed 200 miles away is not what Google wants. The next chapter will show in further depth how staying on top of the changing nature of SEO is the best thing you can do for your business, and outline a framework for how to consider SEO in the context of the modern website.

Charles's Insight

When I was a kid I used to argue with my friends about what superpower I would choose if I could only choose one. Some of my friends thought the power to fly would be the best, some thought to be bullet-proof was a good idea. I don't remember anyone wanting to be good with a lasso like Wonder Woman, by the way. I spent far too much time as a kid dreaming about which of the many superpowers would be the best one. As I think back now I'm pretty sure just to be Superman would be enough; all the other superheroes seemed really ripped off in the superpower stakes.

I have no special skills when it comes to business. I'm not particularly educated, unless you call Grade 9 of high school educated. No one in my family had any money; my family was dirt poor. I never had any relatives with more than $2 to rub together. I didn't have any magical connections. I never got an amazing internship with some entrepreneurial type. I never studied a business subject. I grew up in a country town where the main priority was to simply get a job, and if you did that you would be set for life.

Over the past twenty years I have watched, along with everyone else, the rise of the Internet. Before the Internet you could almost build a business around your listing in the Yellow Pages. Every year you would spend as much as you dared putting in a quarter-page ad to get your phone to ring. I remember spending up to $20,000 dollars on just one ad. Then one day the sales guy from the Yellow Pages came along and offered me the top listing in our niche, online. It was $400 and I remember thinking, "Wow, who will ever use the Internet to get our number?" The promise was that as long as I kept paying the $400 each year I would be the top listing in our category online. The first year, not too much happened; the second year (around 1995) it was like someone had flicked a switch and my $400 got me more phone calls than the $20,000 printed ad. It didn't take too long after that to realise that things were changing fast and the days of expensive print media advertising were over.

The Internet has not only changed the advertising world, it has changed the game generally. Now you can build a good website for a few thousand dollars, less if you have the skills, and bingo, you are in business. I don't care what your business is or what your idea is, there are some keys to making money online; understanding SEO and getting customers to visit and buy from your website is a big one.

But if you want to talk about superpowers—well, I don't really have any. For the past twenty years I have spent most of that time broke or just getting by. However, over the past eight years I have developed a crazy obsession and love for online marketing and Search Engine Optimisation. So in some respects I have just one business superpower; the ability to drive traffic to a website and make money from it.

I now know enough about online marketing and SEO that with any website I build, I know I will make plenty of money from it. In fact, I now make millions of dollars every year from my online marketing strategies. I don't have a traditional business, I work from my home, I spend most of my days by the pool, and I let my websites make me more money than I have ever dreamed of.

If you want to make money from your website, then you need to read and understand this book. By the way, this book is by no means the full story, but it's a start.

In business you need at least one superpower: it can be online marketing, it can be making millions from your website; you just have to know the rules of the game.

Good Luck.

Chapter 2—The Real Magic—3 Golden Keys

Let's get one thing straight; while Bob and Sue are busy considering SEO, they need to be clear from the start: there is no easy, simple, single solution. In order to get to the top of Google and maintain success, you need to consider three key elements equally:

1) Content
2) Links
3) Social media

I call these the 3 Golden Keys and the relationship between these three areas is synergistic; they work in unison and support one another as well as your overall success. Much like making a pizza, something Bob struggles with naturally, it's not just putting your favourite ingredient on it and, presto, you have a great pizza—it's a matter of balance and understanding how all the ingredients contribute to a great taste. Years ago backlinks were the only ingredients needed, and there has been plenty of talk about backlinks being dead. Backlinking or link-building is vital to SEO success, it's just that now you must to do more in order to achieve the same result. I will take you through each step, in turn, to indicate the essential parts you need to consider.

Hey Bob, I know you love mushrooms but do you think we should put some other things on the pizza?

Golden Key No. 1—The Rise of Content

This one is the first because it's fast becoming more important for your online success. Following on from the changes made by Google's Penguin and Panda algorithm updates (discussed in Chapter 3), the focus is clearly placed upon quality content and a comprehensive content strategy. The important change here was the push from clever (often questionable) tactics, to a well-rounded and quality strategic focus, emphasising the production and publication of quality content.

Quality content is more than just the superficial aspects of a page; while it is important to offer elements of a website the people want to actively engage with, you need to first ensure that your content is optimised for SEO so that people can find your website in the first place. This is the focus of the technical SEO areas; ensuring your existing content and all future content is striving towards this common goal.

A unique content strategy should be your focus after you have covered all of these technical elements. The first step to this is a proper understanding of your target market, inclusive of which words, phrases, and keywords (see Chapter 4) they would search for.

When a website is created with its content, more often than not you will find that there are gaps and holes. Bob and Sue have plenty to share about their retreat and getting that message delivered in an effective way is critical. Engaging a quality SEO firm will show you where these missed opportunities are and find the best use of keyword data to correct and get the most out of these oversights. You need to think from the perspective of your market, and then create SEO-conscious content in response.

You are trying to promote yourself in this market, so you should already have a good idea of how to market yourself and what sort of questions should be answered. And rest assured; any quality SEO firm's first steps are always to engage a research team to discover the full extent of your niche area and the potential customer base that you want to appeal to. This means that if there isn't an area being filled, or if there is a question you feel remains unanswered, then you need to have your website take the initiative and create the article, blog post, eBook, or white paper to start the conversation.

The whole process is logical when you think about it; a quality site will lead to more interested traffic, which will lead to an increase in links, and will in turn further the reputation of and positive response to the site. This means that you should always endeavour to have regularly updated content, such as a company blog that has insightful and well-written discussions. The reputation potential is endless; quality leads to more links and, combined with the reach of social media, creates a positive brand, more traffic, more reviews, and ultimately more sales. Your site should not simply sit stagnate, nor should it communicate mundane company updates without elements and insights that a reader would actually value.

'When you start with what's at stake for the buyer,
you earn the right to their attention.'

Jake Sorofman
Gartner Blog Network

This may already be starting to feel overwhelming—you may be feeling a bit intimidated or daunted and just too busy to produce good content 24/7. We understand that you have a business to run. The solution is simple, but not easy: get yourself a writer. If your SEO specialist doesn't offer that service, then find a new company to do your SEO that does provide a well-rounded offering that includes content creation. If you don't want to change your SEO provider then at least find yourself a writer. If you don't have the budget for a full-time writer then at least start off with a university/college student or friend; anyone who can help you get your message down on paper and out the door in all the vast and varied media formats.

When content is created you should always be thinking from the perspective of a potential customer. Ask yourself what they would want to see, and more importantly, what would turn them away. Consider your field, and write accordingly. Discuss content about recent advances in your field, or awards you have been given, as this incites discussion and garners positive reputation. On the other hand, talking about how 'Plan A' is now called 'Plan 1' does not evoke a response and is missing out on its potential as quality, evocative, enticing, engaging content.

'The key ingredient to a better content experience is relevance.'

Jason Miller
Leading Global Content Marketing,
LinkedIn Marketing Solutions

Chapter 8 provides more comprehensive information on the potential content strategies that you should consider implementing.

Golden Key No. 2—Link-Building

A quality link-building strategy is still an invaluable tool for SEO success. Link-building encompasses the SEO tactics that deal with directly creating hyperlinks from external webpages to your own. This serves the purpose of bringing new readers and customers to your website, but also allows for more opportunities for search engine 'robots' or 'spiders' to discover your site for indexing purposes.

The recent changes to the SEO process have placed the onus onto the quality of links rather than the sheer quantity. Thankfully, this means that the days are gone where a new website would deceitfully create a secondary site simply for the purpose of containing thousands of generic links to boost its own success. This has killed the focus of excessive (and ridiculous) link-building and brought it back to a natural, organic, and logical process. It means that a good site needs to be respected not only by its customers, but by its peers. The voice that a site develops in order to attain quality links places a focus back on good practices, good content, and good strategy.

A good way to think of links is as a popularity contest; the more people that know you and that you know, the more successful you will be in winning that contest. The judge of the popularity contest is a computer and it determines your popularity by the people you know. A few years back it was simply a numbers game; the person that knows the most people wins. These days it's still a numbers game but high quality numbers, or in other words, it's more about knowing the right people and connecting with them, rather than just volume. So it goes with link-building; it's still key to improving your website's popularity and ranking online. It still needs to be done, but quality is more and more important. Don't be fooled into thinking it's dead. Backlinking is alive and kicking, so ensure you have a plan to build links or you will slide off the first page of Google and into oblivion.

Chapter 7 will deal with link-building strategies in depth as well as provide a detailed discussion on how to approach the task in the modern SEO context.

Golden Key No. 3—Get Social

That popularity contest example fits well here also; what social media platforms like Facebook, Google+, Twitter, and LinkedIn do for your business, is give your website personality and credibility.

Google sees an active online social life as a key to your relevance online. While it may have taken a while for the traditional SEO gurus to recognise the full potential of social media, recent trends, as well as Google updates, have highlighted the critical role that this field has to play.

They key here is not to simply view social media as a basic platform, or as a way to 'keep up with the competition', but rather, the real winners will be those who can make the best use of this ever-growing phenomenon. Not only does social media allow for an easy, clear, and customer-oriented platform, but it allows you to interact directly with people while building a brand and pushing new customers to your website.

Hey Sue, I've been looking at this Facebook thing for an hour I can't see a wall anywhere!

Every social media strategy is unique; it is dependent upon target market, niche areas, and what you want to achieve. As such, don't feel that you need to go out and get a Twitter account because you think it's what people want to see.

While this area has never been a true goal of SEO until recent years, it is now a critical element for success. If you have approached an SEO firm that overlooks this, then consider it a clear sign that they are not looking towards the future and you won't be getting the flexibility that a professional SEO would guarantee. The types of SEO campaigns that you should look out for are the ones that not only attract new customers through different mediums, but also that raise awareness through organic search results and can ensure customer retention. The power is in strengthening the relationship you have with your customers and ultimately having them feel happy enough to keep coming back to you and referring you to others.

> *'A company that builds a loyal social following has a built-in army to promote their content, day in and day out. That content will get shared, get links, send social signals ... all of which can't be a bad thing.'*
>
> Will Reynolds
> Founder, Seer Interactive

Chapter 9 further discusses the often overlooked and underappreciated role that social media will play in your SEO success.

So, taking into consideration 'The Big 3'—content, links, and social media—you should by now have a firmer understanding of the complex and dynamic system that is in place when it comes to SEO. It may seem a simple notion, but the ways in which you can achieve your website's greatest potential are challenging and often time-consuming. The important thing to remember is to be patient, and to start with the best possible foundation by making sure you know everything you can, and when unsure, bringing in the services of SEO professionals.

> *'Social is the way our work gets discovered. Content that is truly exceptional, unique, and useful can earn tremendous awareness through social media, and that social amplification often leads to great links, which leads to great rankings.'*
>
> Rand Fishkin,
> CEO/Co-Founder of Moz

Moving on, I feel it is important to explore some of the more recent Google algorithm changes to show just how, when, and why things have changed to create the dynamic digital ocean we are currently navigating.

Charles's Insight

If you have a product or a service that you think could make you great money online, then use these golden keys; they will unlock very big doors. Each of these keys is critical to your success online.

The first one is content. I don't care what your budget is, create content. When I first started, I bought some lights and a lapel mic for about $200 and made about twelve YouTube videos. I overcame my fears about being in front of a camera and put together a series of videos. They are not slick, or particularly fantastic, but they have made me at least a million dollars over the past three or four years. The number of people that say, "I saw your video and thought I would give you a call," is mind blowing. The reason I tell this story is, don't just think content is the words you use on your website; it's whatever you can do. Don't underestimate your knowledge. Be radically transparent in what you offer your potential customers online. If you think a simple landing page with nothing more than an image and a phone number is going to satisfy your customers to make a buying decision—you are wrong. Your customers will just go to another site that will answer their questions and you will miss out. So content is king!

Chapter 3—The Arrival of the Google Zoo

What does a Panda, a Penguin, a Hummingbird, and a Pigeon all have in common?

While it may sound like the start of a bad joke, what they have in common is that they are all the latest updates to Google's search engine algorithms.

Google has had a nasty habit of naming its updates after animals, and the latest few have been no exception. But these updates are essential knowledge for SEO practices because it shows how Google has adapted over the last few years to change the way the SEO can be conducted. By learning about these updates, you can get an understanding of what SEO is in 2016, and why the changes have been necessary.

'Google only loves you when everyone else loves you first.'
Wendy Piersall
Author of Mom Blogging for Dummies

Search engine algorithms are based on one basic idea: searchers want the best answer to their questions. Gone are the days when you searched for an electric toothbrush online and found a wealth of information about a new online casino. When a search is carried out there are hundreds or thousands of sites that offer budding links to the query. As a result, search engines needed to figure out a way to bring a searcher the result that they really want, a result that really answers their question. They aim to do this in three distinct ways:

- Ignore all the sites that are irrelevant
- Return a list of sites that meet the search items
- Ensure that those sites are then ranked and prioritised based on relevance

However, there is no simple solution to this process. As such, Google and other search engines utilise complex algorithms that blend together a multitude of factors. The point of these updates is to reward those who are keeping it real. If you sell electric toothbrushes and have a great website about them, you will rank well on Google. The precise formula used is a mystery, but through general knowledge, common sense, and the intention of updates, we can see some of the key topics to consider. These include:

- **Content:** general quality and scope of content, how often new content is generated or updated, relative impact of social media.
- **Keyword metrics:** search for the keyword, keyword mentions, and citations of keywords in relation to specific brands and criteria.

- **Link authority:** the number of reliable, quality links inclusive of trust of linking sites and the anchor text used.
- **On-page factors:** mobile accessibility in the design, load speed for the page, title tags.

As previously mentioned, these factors are constantly changing. This is where Google's zoo of updates comes into play. By understanding the historical trends in what has changed, remained the same, or become forbidden practice, it makes it clearer how best to utilise SEO. And this is where a professional SEO company is key. Many of these professionals have been through these updates and are aware of how times change. By having a professional set up and monitor your service, you can guarantee that you are at the forefront of these changes and you won't be blindsided when Google releases any variations in the future.

Google's Recent Key Updates

Over the past few years, Google has applied a number of updates that have had a particularly drastic effect on site owners. These have focused on three key areas:

- Content and accessibility—Panda
- Quality of links rather than number—Penguin
- The focus on mobile and changing search characteristics—Hummingbird

Taking a closer look at each of these updates, you can be better prepared and know what's needed for you to be up to speed.

Panda

First introduced in February 2011, Google Panda started raising the big questions when it came to discussion surrounding content. The main focus was in eliminating low-quality or thin sites in favour of those with quality, detailed, and consistently updated content. Panda also fought against the sites that manipulated its viewers and clearly prioritised commercial gains over the user experience. Because of the changes to the algorithm within Panda, content marketing has boomed in popularity with a focus on blogging, on-site content, and building off-site content, all with the common aim of improving the general quality of websites.

To help support the general intentions of Panda and show the changing focus, Google released a series of questions with the aim of prompting webmasters to self-evaluate their current practices. Today, we can review these questions to provide a sense of the types of issues that Panda addresses, and the types of violations that are likely to get sites into trouble. The questions included:

- Are the articles short, unsubstantial, or otherwise lacking in helpful specifics?
- Are the pages produced with great care and attention to detail vs. less attention to detail?
- Are the topics driven by genuine interests of readers of the site, or does the site generate content by attempting to guess what might rank well in search engines?
- Does the article describe both sides of a story?
- Does the article provide original content or information, original reporting, original research, or original analysis?
- Does the page provide substantial value when compared to other pages in search results?
- Does the site have duplicate, overlapping, or redundant articles on the same or similar topics with slightly different keyword variations?
- Does this article contain insightful analysis or interesting information that is beyond the obvious?
- Does this article have an excessive amount of ads that distract from or interfere with the main content?
- Does this article have spelling, stylistic, or factual errors?
- Does this article provide a complete or comprehensive description of the topic?

- For a health-related query, would you trust information from this site?
- How much quality control is conducted on content?
- Is the content mass-produced by or outsourced to a large number of creators, or spread across a large network of sites, so that individual pages or sites don't get as much attention or care?
- Is the site a recognised authority on its topic?
- Is this article written by an expert or enthusiast who knows the topic well, or is it more shallow in nature?
- Is this the sort of page you'd want to bookmark, share with a friend, or recommend?
- Was the article edited well, or does it appear sloppy or hastily produced?
- Would users complain when they see pages from this site?
- Would you be comfortable giving your credit card information to this site?
- Would you expect to see this article in a printed magazine, encyclopaedia, or book?
- Would you recognise this site as an authoritative source when mentioned by name?
- Would you trust the information presented in this article?

Penguin

Penguin was Google's answer for cleaning out the underhanded and unfair SEO practices; the so-called 'black hat' tactics. First released in April 2012, numerous updates have been rolled out since then. Up until this point link-building could be manipulated, and various 'link schemes' were developed to take advantage of the grey area of SEO. These included buying links, building thin sites for the sole purpose of linking back to another site, and other similarly unsavoury tactics.

The new dawn of link-building that was ushered in by Google Penguin has required organic link-building to become a more 'above board' process with 'white hat' plans now the best way to succeed in SEO. Because of Penguin, the volume, quality, source, and content of links ultimately fall to the owner of the site. If dubious practices are detected, site owners may be required to conduct an audit of their entire link profile and remove the offending areas. If this isn't complied with, Google is not above banning sites or issuing ranking penalties.

A professional SEO organisation will operate within these new restrictions and create your links in a natural way, which requires time and patience. If there is an offer these days for instantaneous links and speedy

SEO results, don't fall for the trap—it is too good to be true. Today, when building links, an SEO analyst will ask:

- Is this site of high quality?
- Is it relevant to the website's theme/topic?
- What is the site's trust?
- Will the anchor text be beneficial to my site?

Hummingbird

Hummingbird continued the process that began with Google Panda and Penguin, but applied it to two specific dimensions; mobile devices and contextual search.

Principally announced in late 2013, Hummingbird distinctly raised the importance of mobile devices in relation to search. For the first time, mobile responsive designs have been given a clear advantage as they are given an increased importance. This has elevated the need to have a mobile content strategy. The clear assumption now is that readers will be accessing your content from not only a traditional medium, but also a variety of mobile devices including smartphones and tablets. Therefore, there is a distinct benefit to creating your content with a mindset of 'mobile first'.

Contextual search was the secondary aspect of Hummingbird. Prior to this update, the algorithm utilised by search engines would traditionally attempt to identify the most important keywords from a search to interpret an intention. But contextual search allows the context to be seen from the relationship between the terms.

Hummingbird is seen as a logical next step for Google; as technology improves and the ways in which we ask questions become more dynamic, the search engine will adapt too. Searches are evolving from the traditional short keyword-driven searches towards queries being structured the way we naturally speak and ask questions. Hummingbird, quite simply, is helping to guarantee that Google meets the changing demands of its customers.

Pigeon

Google's latest update, affectionately named Pigeon, is the first major update that moves towards local importance. The identified issue was that whenever you would make a Google search for local goods and services, often you would be smothered by nationally (or even internationally) based businesses. With the update, local businesses in a local area rather than the national business with the big AdWords budgets, have a fair chance.

To achieve this, there have been a number of observable changes since its Australian release in December 2014. As Pigeon seems to be about the local area changes, it has changed the order, reduced the number of search results, and focuses on an increased reputation factor. This means that reviews and positive attitudes towards your brand have more of an impact and you will be more likely to appear on the first page. While Google has said, "This new algorithm improves their distance and location ranking parameters," it has done this by changing the search radius, and with this, shrinking an area many businesses have felt left out of. If you are out driving around a strange city hankering for a Krispy Kreme doughnut, all you have to do is Google it and you will more than likely find the closest store nearby at the top of your smart phone's search results. That's the kind of user experience Google wants you to have; usable, relevant, helpful.

As with any update, the focus is placed back on the web owner and developer to ensure they are acting according to the correct practices. It means that the best way to react to these changes is to keep focusing on your strong local SEO campaign and not cut any corners. There is no space to stress one aspect but not another; this is the best way to sustain your efforts while the updates occur. This way, when changes are made you will be flexible enough to adapt where and as needed.

So, it may be time to start thinking even more locally, and begin including neighbourhood indicators in your local SEO strategy.

It's important to make sure you are listed in Google My Business. Make sure you are in all the local directories; Yellow Pages, etc. Make sure you use local suburbs or nearby town names in your content creation.

Google Changes in 2016 and Beyond

Through these changes it is clear that Google is not afraid to modify itself to meet the changing customer base. Google ultimately strives for a more honest and merit-based system.

'The future of SEO is here: understanding and marketing to specific and defined audiences through search engines.'

Adam Audette
Chief Knowledge Officer, RKG

Where it will go next is unknown, but if the past is any sort of indication, you will want to be ready to change with it. This is why a professional SEO company is one of the best places to turn; they can help to make sure that you are at the forefront of the change and that your site is optimised to take full advantage of the current Google algorithm, regardless of the animal.

Charles's Insight

Many years ago when I was learning the value of SEO, I paid about $1,500 per month to one of the country's best online marketing companies. This particular company was well-known in the media as one of the fastest growing businesses in the country; a real success story. After about three to four months they had my website ranking very high on the first page of Google, across a range of keywords. I was excited and money started to come in every day from online sales. I remember asking the owner of the business one day what would happen if I stopped paying the $1,500 per month. He replied that then I would go back to page five of Google and that would be the end for me. Not knowing too much at the time, I remember feeling very uncomfortable about that idea, but the money was rolling in, so hey, what was the problem?

One day—I will never forget this—I did my usual keyword search and my website was gone. I was no longer ranked 1st or 2nd—I was gone. In horror I clicked to page two and still nothing, then page three—nothing. By then it felt like all the blood had left my body and I was in a state of shock. I don't remember what page the website was on but it was bad. In a state of panic I called my SEO Agency and asked what the hell had happened. They mentioned some sort of a Google update and that all their websites had lost rankings. Naturally, it wasn't too much longer afterwards that I stopped paying $1,500 per month to be on page four. I felt I could manage that page on my own.

For those of you that know a bit about the history of SEO, my website had been subject to a major Penguin update, and my agency, who are no longer in business, had simply bought spammy links and paid for traffic. It worked well for a while. They built a multi-million dollar business around it, but when Google changed the algorithm, that was the end of that. The reason this book is important is because even if you 100% outsource your online marketing, you still need to know what's going on. Never lose sight of the fact that it's your business and your livelihood.

Chapter 4—The Keyword Dilemma

If you own a website then you have probably heard of keywords. With the changes made by the Google Hummingbird update, the shift in keyword focus has affected the conceptual basis of SEO and the approach SEO will take in the future.

Five years ago it was a relatively straightforward process; you would start generating keywords from a concept and the process would move logically from there. This keyword list would move the focus of your site's pages, with each focusing on a single keyword, or perhaps a long-tail keyword as you expanded.

However, the times have changed and the modern keyword research process is more complex. I call this the keyword dilemma because it seems, like everything else in the SEO world, that the goal posts are constantly moving. There is one key principle with keywords that applies to most SEO efforts. If your website and social media efforts are naturally in good shape (in other words, good content, backlinking, etc.), then you will be on the right track by default. Google is working hard with all these updates to have the most accurate and relevant keyword search results possible.

So, as we know, Bob and Sue run a health retreat and there are potentially hundreds of keywords they could use to promote their business. It's more than likely that the words 'retreat' and 'health' are far too broad. For that matter the search term 'health retreat' may be too competitive, and depending on how many health retreats are competing for that Google number one spot, it may take lots of work to get traffic to the site organically. If they are the only health retreat in the region then a long-tail keyword like 'health retreat (region/town name)' will rank really well, driving traffic to the site.

Hey Bob, I know you like Chinese food but
I don't think its a good keyword for us.

Conceptual Keywords

Conceptual keywords are one of the ways in which Google is adapting to the changing manner in which people make search engine inquiries. It is where someone might search for a concept rather than the exact item, and the algorithm can decipher the intention based on common search chains. It is a matter of associating the concepts of the search and the logical results and coming to a desired conclusion.

Long-tail keywords are often confused as being concept-based, but these are distinct types. A long-tail keyword is more closely linked with the older style of 'pre-Hummingbird' single keywords. They are representatives of clusters of two, three, or more keywords that follow in sequence. A single keyword may be 'furniture' and a long-tail keyword would be 'ergonomic office furniture Sydney'. The result of the long-tail keyword is that Google will optimise your search results for pages containing all four keywords. The theory behind this is that you will have a narrower search result that is more targeted and likely to fit the need for all the appropriate information contained in a search.

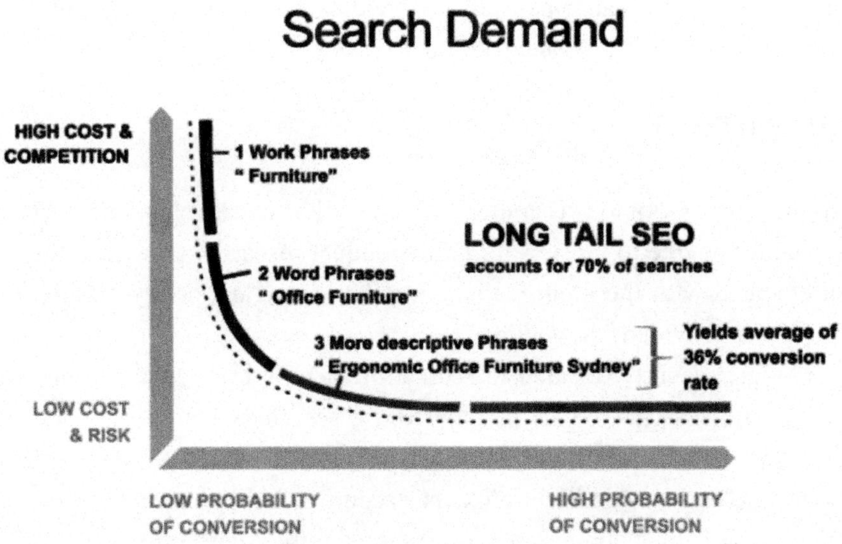

The important part to keep in mind throughout this process is that no matter how well-optimised a site is to conceptual keywords and specialised keywords, the majority of the time the search will be for the core keyword. If you forget to allow for the broader, it is hard to allow for the specialisation. With Google's increasingly sophisticated algorithms allowing for the development of the conceptual search, many new opportunities are being presented to websites to connect with new visitors. This process is also known as LSI Keywords, or Latent Semantic Indexing.

How to Know Which Keywords to Focus On

Regardless of how you plan to structure your keyword research, it all starts with a specific core concept. From this central idea and keyword, you then build a seed list of terms, expanding through interrelated terms and synonyms of your core concept. The expansion of terms will then begin to be tailored towards SEO ideas, content marketing, online marketing, and other considerations. There are a variety of good keyword research tools out there in this day and age, however an SEO company is an invaluable resource. With the changing nature of keywords since Hummingbird, an SEO company will focus upon the research needed in providing the keywords optimised for your needs, taking into consideration a variety of concerns.

(Not Provided)

At one point, Google was content to make all of its searcher keyword data available for free to those wanting to conduct research. However, this has all changed with the modifications made to Google's policy and the role that '(Not Provided)' now plays.

Google recently decided to reduce the access to keyword terms used by specific searchers. This includes those searchers who are logged into a Google account such as Gmail and Google+, as well as anyone using recent updates of Mozilla Firefox. The secure searchers are indicated in the search result site's domain including 'https' rather than 'http'.

According to the (Not Provided) site, www.NotProvidedCount.com, this affects an ever-increasing amount of data, being upwards of 80%. This means that the days of simple and free access to marketing reports through Google Analytics accounts are at an end. Rather, you will need to invest in a Google AdWords advertising account in order to use Google's proprietary information.

Tools for Keyword Research

Some tools are available for keyword research throughout the market to make the process easier. Some are free, but many are not and can be a tad unwieldy. Our recommendation is straightforward—find a tool that works for your site and your needs, and don't be afraid to ask for help. With the changes to the system, the need to have an optimised and diverse keyword plan that features not only a single, simple keyword, but a database of hundreds of imputations of the one term, is now needed in order to optimise your visibility.

Some of the ones to look into include:

- Google Suggest https://support.google.com/websearch/answer/106230?hl=en

- Űbersuggest http://ubersuggest.org/
- Google AdWords—Keyword Planner https://adwords.google.com/KeywordPlanner
- Bing Keyword Tool http://www.bing.com/toolbox/keywords
- Keyword Spy http://www.keywordspy.com/
- Google Trends https://www.google.com.au/trends/explore
- Wordstream http://www.wordstream.com/keywords
- Soovle http://soovle.com/
- SEMrush http://www.semrush.com/
- SEO Book Keyword Tools http://tools.seobook.com/keyword-tools/seobook/
- Google Display Planner https://adwords.google.com/da/DisplayPlanner/Home

5 Deadly Myths About Keywords

Keywords need to be densely packed.

The notion that the frequency of a keyword being used will translate into more success, is outdated. There is no formula relating to the density and consistent frequency of keywords closely packed together. The aim you should bear in mind is to have your specific phrases repeated throughout so that you can maximise their frequency while balancing well-flowing content that evokes a more natural feel and readability.

Optimise only one keyword at a time.

Optimising only one keyword at a time was the strategy circa 2005 and, since all of the updates, can no longer be applied to the market in 2016. If you only focus on the one keyword, then you will find that you have missed a number of opportunities. By diversifying your keyword research you can include the broad elements while focusing your energy on the long-tail terms and the newer focus on conceptual keywords.

Keywords should dominate domain names.

The days of domain names being a long string of nonsensical keywords are thankfully at an end. The keyword-rich domain names no longer have much true value to a domain's visibility. This means that you should focus not on the keywords in your domain name, but can instead start expanding and marketing your brand and focus on brand recognition.

Keyword stuffing is effective.

The overuse of keywords in odd and unusual ways is better known as keyword stuffing. By now you should realise that this is not a practice that would be still supported in the 2016 environment. You should avoid alienating your readers and focus on the subtle and logical way to weave keywords into your copy while still creating excellent and unique content.

Keywords don't matter anymore.

There is also the false idea, with all of the changes that have been made and the shift towards concept-based searches, that keywords don't matter in 2016. This idea is misguided, as keywords play a more important role than ever. It's an evolving market that is constantly changing and developing, so you need to stay on top of the latest changes if you want to succeed. Despite what occurs, keywords will always be at the core of SEO.

The next chapter will discuss some of the possible ways to make sure your on-page elements and design are best suited to the modern SEO environment.

Charles's Insight

A PPC or AdWords campaign will help you learn about which keywords work well in your niche. I remember I spent about a year obsessing about one particular keyword that, no matter what I did, I could not get on the first page of Google. The reason was simple; it was a word that falls into the category of a 'branded' keyword, and Google in spite of all your SEO efforts will never rank a non-branded site ahead of the branded sites. For example, if you sell Yamaha pianos in a retail store in your local community, it would be wonderful if for anyone that searches for 'Yamaha' in your neighbourhood your site will show up, but it probably won't. Potentially if they search for 'Yamaha pianos' you still may not show up. Why? Because Google will generally reserve the 'Yamaha' search ranking result for Yamaha the brand themselves and not just a retailer of that brand. Yamaha is a world-renowned brand name and for Google to put anything other than Yamaha.com at number one would be a real step backwards for a search engine. This is what I mean by branded sites.

However, I came to recognise the magic of long-tail keywords. Once I figured out that I could dominate all sorts of long-tail searches, it was easy to shift my focus. Once I had redirected my strategy the visits to my websites increased massively. So take it from me, living life in the long-tail is very rewarding. Remember—at the end of the day your online strategy is about making money.

Chapter 5—Winning the SEO Game

If you want to make millions from your website then there are some fundamentals you need to get right first. A strong, solid foundation is the key here. To have this, your website's basic structure and the on-site elements of SEO need to be optimised. This concept similarly extends to your design, especially in relation to mobile experiences. (Don't forget the Google Hummingbird update.)

Make sure that you don't get too caught up with the latest developments and the aesthetic elements of the process; you cannot overlook the core components and basic building blocks of your website's foundations.

Case Study—Paid Search Campaigns Increase Markets from Three to Thirteen in Just One Year

Urban Outfitters wanted to replicate the strong brand presence they enjoyed in the UK in other markets throughout Europe. By focusing more on non-branded and localised campaigns, they were able to expand and achieve a strong presence across Austria; Belgium; Denmark; Finland; France; Germany; Italy; Netherlands; Norway; Spain; Sweden; Switzerland; and the UK, and all in just twelve months. Here's how Urban Outfitters achieved the results they did:

- Dividing PPC campaigns into thirteen separate accounts to allow for geographical relevance and localisation within each campaign
- Reducing the reliance on 'branded' campaigns and instead focusing on growing the visibility for non-branded clothing ranges and more generic terms

- Conducting research into each and every local market and building localised PPC campaigns around that knowledge and customer profile

Within twelve months of implementing and maintaining the new localised and non-branded focus, Urban Outfitters achieved the following results:

- 50% increase in conversions across all markets
- 66% decrease in the CPA (cost per action)
- 105% increase in revenue across all markets
- 54% increase in branded campaign conversions (UK)
- 14% increase in branded campaign conversions (EU)
- 102% increase in non-branded campaign conversions (UK)
- 66% increase in non-branded campaign conversions (EU)
- 45% increase in sales numbers via branded campaigns (all markets)
- 93% increase in sales numbers via non-branded campaigns (all markets)
- Expansion into ten new markets in one year

But what do these all mean in dollar terms? This: Urban Outfitters received $12 return for every $1 spent on the paid search campaign.

Two Sides of SEO

It's important to be able to tell the difference between whether an element is on-site or off-site optimisation.

On-site—your content and website infrastructure:

- Keyword cluster research
- Keyword match to existing content
- Keyword match to new content
- Infrastructure, coding, and architecture

Off-site—how other online sources refer to your website:

- Links to your site
- An active and beneficial social media campaign
- Citation profile—references that don't link directly to you

Often more than 50% of SEO elements will be outside of your control, which is why it is best to engage an SEO agency from the start to ensure that the half that can be controlled is optimised to best suit you and your needs.

By investing the time at the beginning of your website's creation, you can determine that the most beneficial tactics are interwoven into your foundation throughout your website's lifespan.

On-Site SEO

Your on-page optimisation is often the elements that are like the hidden stage-hands—behind the curtain, pulling all the levers to ensure the main show continues. It is predominantly a technical enterprise requiring direct and experienced knowledge and can have a demoralising effect because of the sheer amount of patience that is needed.

As with anything involving modern SEO, it takes time to see results. This is why it is critical to know what factors of your on site optimisation have the most substantial effect in 2016.

Local SEO

An especially important on-page element of your business focuses upon a geographic link, a key focus of the Pigeon update mentioned earlier. For instance, if you want customers to be able to approach you, have deliveries, or acquire information specific to your area then you need to ensure they can find you. These elements are inclusive of your Google My Business areas such as Maps, Google+, updating contact details, geographic imagery, and integration with data sources.

Keeping Your Website Updated

The frequency with which your website's content is updated plays a direct role in SEO. A page that is renowned for delivering high-quality, regular, and unique content sees a direct improvement in search engine rankings. One of the quickest and easiest ways to take advantage of this is to incorporate a blog element into your webpage. Make it short, punchy, engaging, and to a schedule you can maintain—then you will be contributing to positive SEO.

Authorship

This is a major contribution to Google visibility. By integrating Google Authorship tools and considerations into how your site is promoted, you can increase your SEO. It draws Google's direct interest to your site because you actively engage Google to identify authors, correlate authorities, curate content, and document the process within your niche area. In simple terms, Google wants a face to put to the website. In the case of Bob and Sue's health retreat, Google wants to know who has put the content and the information on their website. It gives the website credibility, in Google's eyes, when there is an actual person behind the content of the website. Examples of this are when a search returns Google+ business information (including pictures) with Google search results.

Alt Tags

These tags contribute to the identity of your images and assist in the navigation of a site for visually impaired users. Alt tags play an important role in your SEO because they create associations with your images and improve visibility through keywords and the characteristics that Google Image Search seeks.

Heading Tags

These are your H1 and H2 tags. Using natural keyword usage, you can use the heading tags to contribute to the way in which your content is indexed by search engines.

Example of H1:

What makes us the perfect SEO company for you?

Title Tags

These tags serve two key functions; they both assist in keyword search by representing your content, and they are the physical tags that appear in descriptions in the search results. It is therefore ideal to have them both succinct and factual, but also enticing enough to encourage users to engage further with your website.

Example of title tags:

Slingshot Internet Marketing | Internet Marketing

www.slingshotinternetmarketing.com

As a business owner or manager you know that an *online* presence is critical and cannot be ignored right? You also know that there is so much to do to have a...

Creating a Good User Experience

A design should always be in support of, and complimentary to, your SEO—after all, there is no benefit to a brilliant design if you have no traffic for your website. As such, there are a number of areas in which you can focus, both to contribute to ease of search engine access while creating good user experience (UX) for your visitors.

Navigation

A website that is simple and easy to navigate leads to happy users and a happy search engine. This is a matter of basic housekeeping; if your site is messy or too convoluted, then nothing can be found and you will have people losing interest and unable to find your quality content. This is the same consideration with SEO; a cluttered design makes it harder for your keywords and SEO-driven content to be discovered and delivered to potential users.

Advertising

Advertising is often an unavoidable component of most sites, whether it is for external or internal reasons. However, it is important to strike a balance between these ads and your actual content. There is nothing more damaging to a user's experience of a website than obtrusive advertising. Therefore you need to consider how best to strike this balance between a sleek and user-friendly design and your advertising needs.

Interaction

The ways in which a user can interact with your site will affect a variety of factors. As such there is a general benefit to using techniques such as mouse-overs to gain extra benefits. This is an area that allows for the blending of quality graphics and alt text in order to present more information and hit more keyword potential while not compromising a beautiful design. It means that you can add the extra item descriptions or advertise your sales and other calls to action (CTAs) while increasing the potential of your website for search engine Indexing.

Mobile Focus

The Google Hummingbird update introduction placed direct consequences and considerations upon focusing on a mobile-friendly design or responsive design. So you need to consider how your website is viewed on the typical smartphone, tablet, or other mobile device. It doesn't need to be perfect, but as long as there has been a conscious consideration for the mobile market you can see SEO advantages to this process.

Don't forget to make sure that your site has been mobile optimised for a variety of mobile operating systems (OS), including Apple, Android, and

Windows. This is a factor that continues to be an unfolding game-changer, so by allowing for the best view on mobile devices you can take advantage of the changes made by Google Hummingbird while allowing mobile users a more tailored experience.

It's all about trying to maintain the balance between the SEO needs and your aesthetic and business-oriented needs. This can be a challenging process, but by considering the implications of your actions in respect to both areas, you can stay ahead of the game. Once you understand these concepts, it is important to make sure that all your content generation and SEO focus is upon your correct target audience.

Pay-Per-Click Marketing

- Bruce Clay PPC tutorial—outlines PPC basics and provides suggestions
- http://www.bruceclay.com/ppc/pay-per-click.htm
- Google Keyword Planner—PPC keyword research tool
- https://adwords.google.com/ko/KeywordPlanner/Home
- Wordstream—PPC marketing tools and blog
- http://www.wordstream.com/pay-per-click
- Wordstream's guide to choosing a PPC platform
- http://marketing.wordstream.com/How-To-Choose-A-PPC-Software-Platform-Buying-Guide.html
- UnBounce—landing page creator
- www.unbounce.com

Tools from Google

Google offers a number of tools that should be in every SEO toolkit:

- Google Analytics
- http://www.google.com/analytics/
- Google Keyword Planner Tool

- https://adwords.google.com/ko/KeywordPlanner/Home
- Google Webmaster Tools
- https://www.google.com/webmasters/tools/home?hl=en

Local Marketing

- Local SEO guide
- http://www.localseoguide.com/
- Local SEO tools
- http://www.localseoguide.com/local-seo-tools/
- Optimising for local search
- http://www.quicksprout.com/2012/03/26/how-to-optimize-your-business-for-local-search-and-social-marketing/
- Local search tips
- http://blog.crazyegg.com/2013/05/16/local-search-optimization-tips/

Charles's Insight

If you are thinking about your website at this time, wondering if both its on-page and off-page work has been done correctly, then I have achieved what I wanted to in this chapter. The number of wonderful-looking sites I see that are riddled with issues both on-page and off-page is horrendous.

For me, when I first started trying to make money from my websites, I was busy trying to get the colouring right or use really cool images. Do you think Google's algorithm knows the difference between a beautifully photographed image or a blurry backyard photo? Please don't misunderstand me; I'm not saying your website can look bad, otherwise your visitors will bounce right out of there no matter where you are ranked on the first page. It's just that your priorities should be firstly SEO, then look and feel. If I was down to my last $2,000 I would spend it all on my SEO strategy before I would make my site look pretty. It's the traffic that pays the bills, not the aesthetic appeal of the site.

So to sum up this little insight, make sure when you build a website or two you get someone who knows SEO first and web design second. There are all sorts of beautiful pre-designed templates out there so you don't need to look too hard to find them. Finding the templates will take care of the look and feel of the website. It's the SEO component that really matters, and you can't get a template for that. Have a look at the websites in your niche that are ranked in the top three of the first page; you may be surprised at how boring they may look compared to yours.

Chapter 6—The Power of Customer Profiling— Why Profile Your Customers?

Customer profiles are a way to envision and understand your ideal customer. It is a bit like putting together a short story about someone who would be likely to purchase from you, and why. If you don't know who your potential customers are, then a great way to start is by figuring out who has already bought off you. Once you know who your customers are then you will know how to sell your products or services to them. This approach helps to humanise your customers and show that there are a variety of factors that may very well make up their decision-making process, and therefore you need to consider everything you can, such as:

- Basic information
    - Age
    - Gender
    - Income
    - Marital status
    - Geography
- Complex demographic factors
    - Type of career
    - Available income
    - Living situation
- Buying styles
    - Impulse buyer
    - Sales-oriented
    - Research-oriented

- Solution being sought
  - Is there an underlying emotional or mental factor that they might wish your product to solve?
- What they value
  - Brands they might value
  - Benefits that are key considerations in the buying process
  - How they might view the competition
  - What aspects of your product they would value
- Language
  - What language or ways they use to communicate these issues
- Trust
  - What types of endorsements they would trust
  - Customer reviews
  - In-depth discussion
  - Word of mouth
  - Celebrity endorsement
- Advertisement visibility
  - Where are they most likely to come across your product?
  - Shows
  - Publications
  - Social media platforms
  - Where they would spend most of their time

From all of this information, you begin to form a more complete picture of a possible consumer of your products or services.

Let's see if we can help Bob and Sue put together a profile of their perfect customer:

Jenny has a busy professional job in the city. She has a partner and two children and they live in the suburbs near a major capital city. She works long hours, has a mortgage, and helps out at the kids' school when she can. The pressures of work and family are full-on. Occasionally she takes mini breaks with a few girlfriends for the weekend. She is health-conscious and tech savvy. She is forty-two years old.

By starting to think of this information you can begin to see where they would be likely to see your product, and why they would be interested. This can be channelled into further success in the field of SEO.

These customer profiles allow the creation of a baseline persona to represent portions of the audience you are trying to appeal to. It's the ideal way to think of the wide variety of reasons why people would want to engage your services or use your products. It is a concept drawn from the field of market research firms and is ideally suited to SEO, because once you have this information you can tailor your website's physical appeal, keyword search, and advertising to target these ideal markets.

Sorry to interrupt you Sue, do you think we should advertise our retreat on a football website?

Building these profiles gives you a systematic way to discover more about your customers, as well as provide a more direct and responsive task for your marketing team.

Where does this information come from?

The process of building customer profiles is challenging as it requires in-depth research into not only the types of people who would be interested, but which market would be disinterested. The process requires a balance between stereotyping people and realising that you cannot simply place labels on people and expect them to buy. It is a field full of contradictions, and trying to battle this while producing usable results is the key challenge to understanding your audience.

Success comes from three main areas of customer information.

1. Your Information

If you are already an existing business, this process is easier; you should already have a wide variety of information available to you on customer targets, demographics, and buying styles you have retained either actively or passively in the past. If you don't have this, don't panic. It is often the way that you can utilise the information of a generic nature in your chosen niche market, or that of a competitor, and alter it to suit your needs. This provides you with a valuable starting point as well as indicates any gaps in knowledge or information that you can fill with other information areas.

2. Research, Research, Research

Research doesn't need to end at what you have available to you at the current time. You can use all the available tools at your disposal to collect information—social media, publications, and programs that your audience would engage with are ideal starting points. This helps you to realise some of the harder to express ideas of your audience, their viewing habits, what engages them in advertising, how a conversation is structured, and what language they respond to.

3. Talk to Your Customers

This should be an obvious step as well. If you don't know an answer to something, or want to know more about how your customers found out about you, then start a conversation, whether it is in person, through a focus group or survey, or even through an online blog comments section. All of this can yield insights into the interests and desires of your existing customer base and you can then expand on this information with SEO strategies.

However, the best way to make sure you get the results that you want is to engage a professional SEO service. They have the information, knowledge, and know-how to deliver you the desired outcome. While they might not know your industry as intimately as you, they have the connections and experience to pull together the resources from you, your competitors, and other areas, to create the ideal profile of your customers. Sometimes it is about considering the potential Return On Investment (ROI) for these services and realising that a professional start is a better way to succeed.

Your Customers and the 3 Golden Keys

To put audience profiles in perspective, think of it in relation to the 3 Golden Keys to SEO: content, quality links, and social media presence. Creating a beneficial and relevant catalogue of audience profiles will both inform your expansion of these three areas, and identify problems that you are yet to consider.

Content

As we established in Chapter 2, a good content strategy is key to success. But make sure that your content is considering the people you wish to target. If your content doesn't align with your target market, your content will be unsuccessful. Have your customer in mind when you put together your content. A great question to be asking is, "What problem am I solving?" Your customers will look to your content to solve their problems.

Links

By knowing more about your target audience, you can develop the quality links that boost your SEO efforts. Think about it: if you identify that your audience would primarily visit a specific site to gain their information, then advertisement and link-building that targets this site will be immensely beneficial. The other side of this is that instantly these sites that you choose will have the reputation and trust that you want associated with your website. Combining these efforts is seen in both search engine results and your audience building. Make sure your SEO agency or staff members fully understand what your customer profile is. For Bob and Sue, advertising in a football magazine or website would be insane—last I checked, forty-two-year-old professional women don't read them, so having links built from that site would be missing the point.

Social Media

By knowing what sort of social media appeals to your customers, and what sites they engage with, you can customise your social media SEO campaign. This will see direct results in whichever networks you are active in, what content you create, the style and tone you take, and what engagement you seek from your audience. Use your social media to build a community; you may want to offer some freebies, or run a competition to start getting your potential customers engaged.

The Role of Keywords and Your Audience

By now you should realise that the connection between understanding your audience and choosing the right keywords is important. The keyword searches that a Google user will use are highly individual and reflect not only intentions, but vocabulary. Sometimes it can be a simple matter of understanding how two people would discuss a similar product; for example, 'SEO services' and 'website help'—while both terms may actually apply to the same product, if you don't have an understanding of the type of wording your customer would use then you may miss a valuable opportunity. By understanding your audience, you can take the huge quantity of keyword possibilities and filter them into what your customers would be most likely to use. By prioritising you can specialise your focus and save on wasted efforts.

Why a Customer Profile Might Fail

Often in the marketing world you will see that customer profiles will be generated at a large expense only to sit idle and have no direct role. This occurs when the profile has not been created properly, or has been created simply to tick a box and move on. Some of the reasons for this failure include:

Poor Data Foundation

If your data is not real, or is skewed by poor results or bias, then your information is useless. You need to be focusing on the deep and actionable insights into the minds of your customers or you will only have a superficial, perhaps even inaccurate representation that is doomed to fail.

Profiles Are Not Versatile

If the profile is not well-rounded then it cannot be expected to represent the actual body of your customer base. This stems from problems with limited or poorly retrieved sources for your customer base. Again, if a profile is not versatile and flexible, then they are just basic words on a page and cannot represent your true customer. The best solution to this is to engage the services of someone with experience in this area of sales (even better if the company is SEO-oriented), so that you know that the drafted profile will be a dynamic, living embodiment of your actual audience.

Too Much Data, Not Enough Life

If you have your profile simply as a list of dot points about age, gender, and income, then they are just another lot of statistics and not a profile. This 'soul' in your profile is what helps to show the motivations for the customer, how they shop, how they think, and what they want. If you are limited in the meaningful analysis then your team can't be inspired into insights and the usefulness of these profiles will be short-lived.

Focus Shifts

Some companies don't use the profiles to their fullest potential because they don't value the insights they provide. If you are simply doing this as a task to tick off the to-do list and move on, then no matter how good your information is, you won't receive the benefits. This comes down to culture and education; if you value this process, your team will value it, and it will be treated with the respect needed to actually see results.

By now it should be clear that an in-depth and comprehensive understanding of your audience is critical to any business and essential to a successful SEO campaign.

The next step is about link-building practices. The next chapter will discuss this in depth as well as how the current SEO updates have influenced attitudes and what you should look for in an effective strategy.

Charles's Insight

You could spend an enormous amount of time trying to please everyone in your business. Here is an easy thing to do that will help you know exactly how to grow your business and attract the right sort of customer. It's called the Pareto Principle, or the 80/20 rule. If you're not sure who your perfect customer is or how to profile them, or you just simply don't have the resources to analyse what's going on, then just do this: take a look over the last twelve months of sales in your business, make a list of the customers that contribute to 80% of your revenue, and then profile them. I can promise you that 80% of your revenue is not coming from 80% of your clients; in most cases it's probably coming from the top 20% of your clients. Now here is another thought for you. I also bet that the top 20% of your customers are the lowest maintenance customers you have. It's more than likely that your most painful, time-consuming customers who take up most of your time are in the bottom 20% of your revenue. I'm going to refer to this top 20% of your customers as the 'Top 20' and that profile of customer as the 'Top 20 Profile'.

If you are can relate to what I'm saying, then smile, because I have some amazing news for you. Think about this: if 80% of your revenue comes from only 20% of your customers, then all you need to do is market to the Top 20, build a profile that fits the Top 20 Profile, and go for it. The only reason you are putting up with the customers that give you grey hair and seem to complain daily and spend so little, is because your marketing is failing. The only reason you are dealing with those high maintenance, small spending customers is because you don't have enough of the good customers. The only reason you don't have enough good customers is because your marketing isn't doing enough to get you the Top 20. I know this smells like pointing out the blatantly obvious—and it is!

If you want to make millions of dollars online I'm going to let you in on my biggest secret. Years ago I started a website; I spent about $3,000 building it. At the time it was a lot of money. I was busy running a few other businesses at the time so I didn't pay too much attention to it. After about six months of doing SEO and running a PPC/AdWords campaign from the site I discovered something amazing: the average sale in dollar value from this site was about $3,000 dollars. I also discovered what sort of customer was spending the lowest amounts on the site as well as the profile of the customer spending far more than $3,000 dollars. The only problem was that I didn't make many sales; it was just here and there. Up until I had profiled my perfect customer for this site the fact that it just ticked along making the odd sale didn't really bother me, as I had other things going on.

It was around about this time that I was selling one of our businesses that I thought I really should invest more time into this website, since it had great potential. I could see enormous potential; it was almost a perfect passive income, I just needed to increase my sales. At the time I was marketing to my local area with just one website. I then imagined what it would be like to market to 150 local areas with 150 different websites. Logically you would think that would work, right? I woke up the next morning and registered over 150 domains and had my team start on building 150 uniquely local websites across the country. From there we completed the SEO on all of those sites, and guess what? I increased my sales by forty per cent—the only reason it's not 150 per cent is because some areas are not as big as the one I started from. Now you need to know there are rules that Google and other search engines have about adopting this strategy and you need to know them before you try this idea—but if you do it right, it will work. In other words, it's simple; practise on one website, learn how to make a buck, and then repeat. I still make millions from these sites. It's not rocket science. Rich people for thousands of years have adopted this strategy. It may come as a surprise to you to know that most industries have these kinds of monopolies. Coca Cola own a huge range of drink brands, yet none of us seem to mind too much. When you are thirsty you go to the 7Eleven and buy a drink—whether it's a Coke, Vitamin Water, or bottled water, chances are you're buying from the overarching brand that is Coca Cola.

If you are making money with your website now, just consider building a monopoly on the first page of Google. Do you really want your potential customers to buy from your opposition?

Once you have done that, guess what you do with that pesky bottom 20% of your customers? Refer them to your opposition and stop wasting your resources.

Chapter 7—The Art of Link-Building

Links have always been an essential element of SEO, but with the prominent rise of social media and other marketing elements that have in the past encouraged the use of 'black hat' tactics, it can be easy to see why the importance of links may have been removed and why people may be scared at the idea of making it a part of their SEO strategy.

Don't be deceived; link-building is still crucial and if you want to succeed online you better have a strategy in place. There is just more to do these days.

The idea that link-building is dead and buried may have been true a few years ago, but with the recent Google updates, especially Penguin, the problem has been addressed and the current environment for link-building is more honest and focuses not on sheer numbers, but on quality links—it is now all about 'link earning'.

'The objective is not to 'make your links appear natural'; the objective is that your links are natural.'

Matt Cutts

Do you have any ideas on what a quality link is Sue?

The Successful Link-Builder

As mentioned, the rollout of Google Penguin in 2012 has had a serious and deep-rooted impact on how links are considered in SEO. It has created a shift from schemes to strategies. Pre-2012, the SEO focus was upon manipulating the search engine algorithm by generating as many links as possible from a variety of domains, and little attention was given to the quality of links, sites, or anchor text. This led to a new generation of incestuous SEO practices, such as link wheels. When Google said 'enough!', much of the fallout led to the collapse of these sites and the eradication of these practices. These techniques, while well-established, became known as 'black hat' tactics. A long list of approaches soon became not only unpopular, but counter-productive.

To give you an indication, here are some tactics that are (thankfully) dead in the world of 2016 SEO:

- Abusing blog networks
- Buying links
- Link wheels
- Trading links
- Low quality or irrelevant sites providing links
- Anything from a source that resembles spam (excessive comments, article marketing, etc.)

Link-Building in 2016

So, in the 2016 SEO universe shaped by Google Penguin, the process is harder, slower, and more challenging—so how can this be a good thing? Firstly, by removing all the underhanded and shady practices, it means that to get results you need to be a website that actually produces quality content and earns links to similar quality. It is about building a true reputation and earning an authentic place at the top of the search engine results rather than manipulating your way to the top.

As such, you need to look at the following ways to not create links, but earn links:

- Promote content appropriately so the best types of people are exposed to it. They will be more naturally motivated to share and link your content.
- Focus on relationships; if you have influence in your professional sphere then you will build a reputation for quality and you will be turned to for your expertise and value.
- Content that is original, engaging, and fascinating to your audience will lead to people naturally wanting to discuss, comment on, and share your website.

There is still a level of strategy to this process, but you start to see more merit rather than manipulation. No longer is it a numbers game; the focus is on quality and value. You should now build your brand, not your links. If you do this naturally then the link strategy will flow logically as a by-product of your work.

'Running with the herd is not always a great idea; be unique, and the links will come.'

Debra Mastaler
President, Alliance-Link

If you are unsure of how to proceed with this, then approach an SEO professional. If they are willing to see the potential in your website and services, then they often have the connections and trust that can help to create the quality links that your site needs to get the respect you believe it deserves.

The Quality Link

The answer to this was provided by the Google Penguin update. A number of questions began being introduced as a sort of guide to the type of links that a webmaster should be seeking or asking before engaging a link profile. The following list shows the important considerations you make in determining the quality of a potential link.

- Is the site relevant to the theme of my content?
- How much advertising does it have; has it been overrun?
- Checking the comments and social media presence, does the site have an active community?
- Is the content that it publishes of a high standard?
- Is the development and selection of content being driven by a positive editorial hand?
- Is their incoming link profile of a high standard?
- Is it a professional design/site?
- Ultimately, am I happy having this brand associated with my own?

If you begin to make the conscious change towards earning the links, rather than generating them, the quality of your website and the respect that it earns can only exponentially increase.

Link-Building Tools

- Ahrefs—backlink checker and analysis tool
- https://ahrefs.com/

- BuzzStream—link research and link-building tool
- http://www.buzzstream.com/
- GSA search engine Ranker—niche backlink-building tool
- https://secure.avangate.com/order/product.php?PRODS=4555684&QTY=1&AFFILIATE=48198
- Inspyder Backlink Monitor—backlink analysis tool
- http://www.inspyder.com/products/BacklinkMonitor/Default.aspx
- Link Emperor—tool used to build authority links
- http://www.linkemperor.com/?a=ec6ce75b4ecf
- Link prospector—helps users build targeted backlinks
- http://linkprospector.citationlabs.com/
- Majestic SEO—backlink checker and site exploration tool
- http://www.majesticseo.com/
- Open Site Explorer—discover new linking opportunities
- http://www.opensiteexplorer.org/
- Rankwyz—link-building tool
- http://www.rankwyz.com/
- ScrapeBox—pinging, commenting, link-building tool
- http://www.scrapebox.com/

The next chapter will address one of the key ways to try and expand in this direction; content marketing.

Charles's Insight

I have over hundreds of websites ranked at number one on Google. Without a link-building strategy you may never get your website to number one—this is fact. This is not something I recommend you do yourself. It's not that you cannot do it, it's just that it's very time-consuming and outsourcing it is the logical choice. Naturally I recommend using www.slingshotinternetmarketing.com to help you do this because it's my company, but seriously, get a link-building strategy in place. Make sure whoever you are using is not buying links or doing other crazy things like that. There are simple winning strategies with link-building that should be getting you great success. This particular aspect of SEO is getting some very bad press lately and the reason is simple; we are buying into the Google rhetoric. Google makes the rules of the game and Google doesn't want you to link-build in any way other than naturally.

Now ask yourself these questions: what is a natural link and how often would you as a business owner create a link? Do you have an answer in your mind yet? When was the last time you posted on someone's blog or listed your site on a directory? Let me just spell it out for you: after Bob and Sue, our health retreat owners, finish a thirteen-hour day toiling away—running classes, paying bills, checking clients in and out, managing staff, finding a minute to eat—do you think they then post a few comments on some industry website and link it back to their website? The answer is obvious, right—never, or rarely.

OK, now you know that links are important, don't go onto www.fiverr.com (a great website, by the way) and find someone in India to create 5000 backlinks for you either; that is not the answer. With that strategy, more than likely you will end up with more penalties than you can jump over. Just find someone or some agency that knows what they are doing so that you can naturally generate the right sort of links in the normal amount of time.

Chapter 8—Content is King

Today, high quality content is the foundation of good SEO and is essential to making the most of building links, social media campaigns, and, overall, creating goodwill for your brand. While in the past content may have had a less prominent role, with the current Google algorithm changes brought in by Panda and Penguin, the focus upon quality, regular, and unique content is ever-increasing.

There are some key ideas to consider when you are putting content onto your website. The first and simplest rule of thumb: is it good content? Will your customers want to read or engage with what you are saying? The notion here is that the quality content drives your appeal to customers and their interactions with you, your content, and your brand; and your overall success. When dealing with this inbound marketing focus, it is imperative that there is a focus on creating strong content for your website, social media, and email campaigns. If this is done well, you will build your reputation consistently and will have more ability to influence your audience into action and interaction with your business.

You may be thinking, "I don't want to give too much away; my competitors might steal my ideas!" Of course you need to use common sense here, but by and large your competitors already know all that you know and maybe even more. What good, informative content does is build confidence with your potential customers that you know what you are talking about.

'Determine the biggest problem facing your buyers and create a resource that solves that problem'

Jay Acunzo
Director of Platform and Community, NextView Ventures

Be radically transparent. This may seem counterintuitive, but think about the websites you have saved as a favourite or bookmarked. I can assure you it's because they are giving you information beyond your expectations and you don't want to lose track of them. They are fountains of knowledge, so to speak. Your customers are no different; they need the information now, that's why they are online.

So What is Content?

Content is a broad and expansive term given to the aspects of your website that your customers and audience can view and interact with. This can be visual, literary, or even extend beyond the website into everyday events or activities.

'Content is the atomic particles of all digital marketing.'
Rebecca Lieb, Analyst, Altimeter Group

Content includes, but is not limited to, the following:

- Images, pictures, gifs
- Web page content
- Written articles
- Blog posts
- Guest Posts
- Social Media updates and content
- eBooks
- Reports
- Brochures
- Catalogues
- FAQs
- Videos
- Animations

It's important to choose a broad range of content that can aid you in engaging with your audience while still creating a balance and flow that you want your brand to represent. One way to do this is by experimenting with different ways to find your brand's voice. For instance, if you haven't thought about animation, perhaps approach someone and get an idea of what they could do for you. Research the possibilities and don't be afraid to keep trying different ideas until you find the approach that is not only right for that particular situation, but right for your business.

On-site and Off-site Content

Content creation doesn't have to stop at your website; the creation of off-site content is an interesting and useful way to expand your brand and add to your link profile and audience. This opens you up to a new area of success. If you are writing great content then you should try to share it around by publishing both on-site and off-site to maximise exposure.

Make sure you keep the best content for your own website—that is the content that is keyword-rich and engages with the audience, but there is no harm in having some pieces externally bringing in more interaction with your website. This off-site content is one of the best ways to build visibility for your brand and create a name for you that is synonymous with quality content.

But be warned; often people go too far with this, as was seen in the trend of guest blogging a few years ago. Don't choose all opportunities, choose the right ones.

Guest Blogging: Useful, or a Trap?

Guest blogging has been a trend that has been growing in popularity over the past few years. It was a simple idea; one site would offer to blog quality content on another in the same field so as to add content to one page while bringing support to the other. It seems to be a mutually beneficial arrangement, and relatively harmless. However, this technique was quickly exploited. This seems to be the recurring theme with many aspects of SEO over the past few years; once some people find an easy solution, it is stretched and abused until Google finally cracks down on it.

While this has not yet happened, there has been various calls to stop the shady practices and start creating quality content. If the shady industry taking advantage of this continues to abuse the system, then it can only end poorly for those people. The thing to always remember with Google is that it only tends to forbid the abuse of practices. It would never remove guest blogging, but would rather seek to regulate the quality. As such, the best thing for you to do is to focus on quality. If you are producing low-quality blogging on low-end sites then this will get you nowhere. If, however, you produce quality content with reputable sources, then this will only improve over time—even if changes are made through Google, you shouldn't feel their wrath.

You should always be focusing on the big picture here. The best part of guest blogging is not the links that you can make, but rather the increased exposure that you can achieve. As such you need to make sure you put your best foot forward and represent your brand to the best of your ability. If your blog is a piece of literary garbage then how can you expect your audience to trust or respect your business? It all comes down to this focus on quality; this drives traffic, interest, and interaction. You need to be conscious of the decisions that you make and decide wisely when choosing who you want your brand associated with.

I thought I read on your blog that this class was lots of fun?

How to Promote Your Content

It is not enough to simply have quality content sitting on your website if no one knows that it is there. As such, make sure you invest your time and efforts into a content promotions strategy. It is true that although organic searches will eventually discover your content if your keyword and link profiles are sufficient, there is a better way to go about it: strategic promotion. The aim here is to get two distinct results: first, interaction through likes and shares that contribute to your organic performance, and second, decreasing the need to rely solely on a search engine to bring in traffic.

So, to do this, here are some different approaches to take with your strategic promotion campaign:

Newsletters

If you have a newsletter, ensure that it is updated regularly, and focus on producing quality and engaging content. You don't want these to simply sit unread by your subscribers. A way to approach this would be to look into various programs that provide feedback and data on newsletter engagement. And ultimately, you don't want subscribers who were conned into signing up—rather you want them eager to hear the latest news from your business.

Social Media

There are various avenues for content promotion through social media, both paid and unpaid, but this can be as simple as driving the focus towards a 'call to action' or including links and quality content for your followers to share.

Join the Conversation

One of the best parts of social media is the ability to join and contribute to the wider conversation that may be going on in your industry. It will let you know more about the latest information and decisions as well as how your target audience would be responding to various changes. One way to know how to tailor your efforts would be to look into websites such as hashtags.org.

Target Those with Influence

If you are engaging with your specific industry or market sphere, you should have a bit of an idea of who some of the more prominent people in your industry are and who has an element of influence. This could vary from competitors, to experts in the field, or even critics. When you are producing quality content, sometimes a personalised message to these figures could help to not only get more exposure, but even endorsements of your efforts.

Link it All Together

When publishing any content, whether on-site, off-site, in your newsletter, or on social media, don't just tie it back to the website, but draw attention to the other content you have. A good way to do this would be to periodically publish a highlights version of your content.

While it may seem crazy to say in a book about SEO that you need to look beyond SEO, it makes a lot of sense. It should be apparent by now that SEO is more encompassing than just keywords and links. You need to have a comprehensive strategy going forward across a number of platforms and fronts so as to build your visibility and brand. And besides, every effort you make to raise awareness of your brand supports the efforts of a professional SEO campaign, and vice versa.

I'm not sure we should be publishing our bank balance on our blog somehow.

Content Marketing and Copywriting Tools and Resources

- Addvocate—content sharing platform for companies
- https://addvocate.com/
- Convert—A/B testing for more effective content
- http://www.convert.com/
- Copyblogger—tools and resources for content marketers
- http://www.copyblogger.com/
- Curata—content creation software
- http://www.curata.com/
- Inbound Writer—content performance and analytics software
- http://www.inboundwriter.com/
- Optimizely—A/B testing for more effective content
- https://www.optimizely.com/
- Outbrain—content curation
- http://www.outbrain.com/select
- Papershare—content generation platform
- http://www.papershare.com/
- Parse.ly—predicts content performance with audience
- http://www.parsely.com/
- Percolate—content marketing platform
- http://percolate.com/
- ProBlogger—building a better blog
- http://www.problogger.net/
- Scribe—content marketing software by CopyBlogger
- http://scribecontent.com/
- SEOBook—optimising your blog
- http://www.seobook.com
- UberFlip—content hub creation
- http://www.uberflip.com/

Our next chapter will discuss the elements of a successful social media campaign in greater detail.

Charles's Insight

Be creative! That is probably the best advice I can give anyone when it comes to creating content online. YouTube videos, blogs, podcasts, white papers, explainer videos, testimonials, updates—and the list goes on. Personally, for me, it has been easier to do things in batches. For example, if you are going to make a video where you are explaining a product or service in front of a camera, plan to put together ten of them, all on different subjects. By the time you set up the camera and lights, you don't want to shoot just one video, it's too time-consuming.

Write a book! This is by far the best advice I would give anyone when it comes to growing your business. I will give you three amazing reasons.

1. It sets you apart from your competitors as an expert
2. It will give you some serious credibility with your potential customers
3. You will have enough content to last for years with what you have written

For every business owner the problems are all the same; no money and no time. You may be thinking, How can I write a book—that will take months, right? It doesn't have to, and you don't have to write every word yourself. By writing a book you will have a solid and cohesive content foundation. You will never have to rack your brains for a new idea every time you need to put something up on your blog or social media or in your monthly newsletter.

Chapter 9—
How to Be Likeable—Social Media

The role that social media plays in SEO has long been a matter of discussion and debate. The main question is whether it can actually have any real impact. In short: yes, it can.

Think about social media; it is a rapidly expanding social platform with which to engage with your audience in a human and responsive manner. To put it all in perspective, there are over 1,413,000,000 active Facebook users, over 1,113,000,000 active Google+ users, and over 305,000,000 active Twitter users with, on average, 9,253 tweets per second. This is an enormous quantity of information being accessed and created by people from a diverse and easily accessible platform.

For Bob and Sue and most small business owners, their social pages like Facebook, Instagram, Google+, and LinkedIn are pretty easy to update and maintain even for the most computer illiterate out there. A weekly update on these pages is not a huge task. It puts a face to your business. Just a word of warning: a great rule of thumb is to make sure that whatever you put up there is something that you would actually want to read. Don't put what you had for breakfast on your Facebook page—no one cares! (Unless of course your breakfast relates to your brand, e.g. as a dietician, fitness guru, chef, etc.)

Hey Sue, do you think I should put a picture of our new water cooler in the yoga room on our Facebook page?

Social media doesn't act in the same way that a normal page does. This is because social signals from Twitter and Facebook are not used by Google. This is because, if it did, problems would arise if Google's attempt to index the pages was blocked by Facebook and Twitter for privacy reasons. But for the most part, social media pages are treated the same as any other site's pages; but there a few exceptions to this treatment as well. The issue with social media is at first confusing, but I hope to make it clear exactly why this is a key principle in modern SEO.

> *'Social media marketers that partner with their search marketer counterparts are finding success by focusing on the content that fuels social media activities and analysing trends to unlock opportunities and maximize impact and revenue.'*
>
> Jim Yu
> CEO, BrightEdge

There are a number of key benefits that a solid social media presence can bring to a company that takes this area seriously in their SEO campaign. Some of these more significant benefits are:

Increased awareness of your brand.

If you use social media strategically and on the right platforms, you can grow your brand. It is a fantastic way to join the conversation in your industry, introduce your name to potential customers, and start building the sorts of relationships that will grow your business.

Makes you seem more human.

For the most part, you want to create a face of professionalism so that your company gets the respect that you want at the top of its field. However, through social media presence, you can balance the professionalism with an ability to talk to your customers on a human level that they can respect. It lets conversations evolve more naturally and organically, which can have good results.

Responsiveness of social media.

Because of the nature of social media, you have the ability to respond to and listen to any feedback to your product and services. This allows you to harness the value of the two-way conversations and interact with your customers. You can engage in practices of 'social listening' so you can monitor your brand and even influence the products you release or the stylistic changes you make.

Word-of-mouth marketing.

By using social media, you can further your campaigns and events through simple word-of-mouth. If it is exciting enough, or original and engaging, a natural process of sharing and commenting will spread the word through an engaged social media audience.

Unique medium to communicate.

The concept is one that is truly unique. It is a low cost, low barrier, simple method to directly communicate with your customers. It is a brilliant way to reach out, whether because of a sale, announcement, or just day-to-day activities. An active social media presence can provide cheap and easy marketing.

Customer loyalty.

Social media can build your reputation, and by extension, customer loyalty. As you gain more recognition and trust as a quality and reliable company, customers who are regularly exposed to your brand through social media will more deeply interact with you and your updates and develop the loyalty that translates into sales.

Customer trust.

Because of the nature of social media, you can be viewed as a more trustworthy and contactable business entity. This makes it feel like you are more accountable and that you care more about your customers. This is especially true if you are a company that has a purely digital presence.

Google+

Google+ is undeniably a social media tool of growing importance. Despite the fact that it has been denied that Google+ has any unfair advantage over any other social media networks for SEO purposes, you should take the time to maintain a presence. You may also argue that no one uses it, including you. If your goal is to rank well in Google however, this one is critical. It can't be denied that the information and content used on Google+ can be more directly beneficial for your rankings over the long term because of the close relationship between Google and Google+. This is mainly because of the professional value that many people place on social networks for vetting purposes, and while LinkedIn is the predominant source here, it applies to all forms.

So if you are looking to get started with Google+ you should look into the following:

- If you are a business, claim your page on Google+ or set up an account for a personal enterprise
- Begin customising your profile to grow your brand
- Add information about your business such as contact details and locations
- Add and connect to your contacts through Google+ circles
- Maintain a presence through scheduled regular updates and contributions

What Social Media is Best for My Business?

If you spread yourself too thinly across all social networks then it is hard to maintain a quality presence. As such you should place your focus in the areas that will best benefit your business. There is a wide range of networks out there, including the mainstream platforms like Twitter, Facebook, Google+, Pinterest, YouTube, Instagram, and LinkedIn. But don't forget to look into some of the smaller niche areas that may be specific to your industry. When considering where to invest your time, think about the following:

Communication Style

There are some formats that will be better suited to the image you wish to create. As such, you need to think about how exactly you want to communicate: do you have images and designs? Insights and words? This will determine whether you turn to blogs, or a visual site like Pinterest. For example, if you make wedding cakes, Pinterest, Instagram, and Facebook all have a visual communication style and would work for that kind of business. If you run an accounting firm, Pinterest and Instagram are going to be less effective—unless of course you can get some great photos of your calculator!

Your Target Market

Once you know where your audience invests their time and energy, target this social media network. There is no point in having a presence somewhere that won't be seen by the people you want to do business with. If your target audience is middle-aged male executives then maybe Pinterest is not the place for you to spend a significant chunk of your marketing budget, simply because generally not too many men in that age bracket know what Pinterest even is, let alone use it.

Natural Connections

Sometimes one platform will just have a more natural affinity to your business model or brand style. If this is the case, then utilise this platform as it's more likely that you will be able to reach like-minded people and achieve the best level of engagement.

Content is Linked to Social Media

Social integration is one of the best ways to spread your content and gain visibility. If you share and spread your content, not just on your website, but through social media as well, it is clear to see that it is more likely to be seen, read, and shared. When doing this, don't forget the power of sharing features, topical tagging, and quality content that will start a conversation and add something of value that people will want to actually see and share.

'Content Marketing has become the catalyst that fuels search and social media activity.'

Jim Yu
CEO, BrightEdge

Google+ and Google Authorship

One of your focuses should be on the Google+ region of social media. As it stands there is no direct advantage to Google's social media over any other (i.e. algorithm favouritism). There are advantages because of the way that Google can use this information to your advantage. Google's Authorship connections are always going to be important for your visibility and content awareness.

Driving Connections through Social Media

Social media will constantly be used to make connections with both your audience and those in your profession, so don't forget to mingle where you can. The other important part that drives connections is the diverse range of expression, so feel free to take advantage of sites like Pinterest and YouTube and express your content in a range of multimedia and unique forms.

So by now you should be clearly grasping how important social media can be when you use it to your advantage. Our next chapter will discuss how all these elements (content, links, and social media) can then start to come together to work towards building your brand and giving you a voice.

Remember to have fun with this also. It may sound strange, but remember: being social is not just all about business. If you happen to have something interesting to share even if it's off-message that you think your social fans will love, then post it up there; create a conversation and engage your fans.

Social Media Marketing Tools and Resources

- Hootsuite—content management, engagement tracking, scheduling platform
- http://www.hootsuite.com/
- Jon Loomer—advanced Facebook marketing blog http://www.jonloomer.com/
- Mention—social sentiment/brand, name mentions tracker https://en.mention.com/
- RazorSocial—social media marketing blog http://www.razorsocial.com/blog/
- Social Media Examiner—tips for using social media for business
- http://www.socialmediaexaminer.com
- Social Media Marketing Magazine—industry publication for social media marketers http://www.smmmagazine.com/
- Social Mention—sentiment tracking, analytics http://www.socialmention.com /
- SocialMouths—social media marketing blog http://socialmouths.com/blog/
- SocialOomph—fully integrated platform, allows you to schedule content across networks, track mentions, engage with followers, etc. https://www.socialoomph.com/
- Twazzup—Twitter monitoring http://www.twazzup.com/
- Tweetdeck—engage with Twitter followers in real-time, track mentions and engagement https://tweetdeck.twitter.com/

Charles's Insight

There is no denying that social media is a powerful tool in your online toolbox. How you use it is the difference between success and failure. I remember the first Facebook competition I ran years ago; we gave a $300 prize to the person who got us the most likes on our page. Looking back now I think that's pretty funny, but at the time we were amazed at the results—the winner of that competition had over 600 of her friends like our page.

Things have come a long way with social media and one of the best things is that generally it is something you can contribute to for free and you can build loyal customers by doing so. A powerful idea with social media is to identify what your customers and potential customers care about and give them small but regular doses of it. For example, in the case of Bob and Sue, a really simple idea Sue could use would be to take a photo of one item she would recommend for their customers to buy as part of their weekly groceries that would make life healthier and better, whether it's a drink, food, body product, or just anything she feels her customers would be interested in. Sue could pop the image up on Instagram, post it on her business page wall with Facebook and Google+, and finally, maybe tweet about how cool it is. This idea is not expensive and doesn't take that much time but will build trust and loyalty from her customers. Don't just use your social media as an advertising platform to blast everyone with your latest product or sale; it will get old pretty quickly for your customers and followers (potential customers). Instead, engage with them. Maybe Sue could ask her customers what soap they use, so their skin doesn't get too dry. She could take a photo of her soap and start a discussion about the subject. Remember, it's not an opportunity to advertise, it's an opportunity to engage your audience and build on your brand's reputation.

Having said that, be careful to not get too far off topic—don't start posting 123 photos of your cat every week or the only audience you will have left are cat lovers and maybe your mum.

Chapter 10—Branding Essentials

Brand recognition, and the ability to build your brand through SEO, is always increasing in importance. The general consumer focus has shifted towards a combination of building general brand awareness and having a product that genuinely speaks to them. This means that if a customer has heard of your brand favourably, then they are far more likely to purchase or engage with your services, then that of your competitors.

If your business is 100% online then this step is critical, crucial, and imperative; it's that important. All you have to build trust and credibility with your customers is your website. Remember, the best SEO strategy in the world won't help a website that is poorly designed and is about as user friendly as a second-hand lawnmower. Despite all the talk about metrics and Google algorithms, your actual customers are human beings with needs. Get the message right on your website and people will spend time on it and bookmark it, re-visit it, and tell their friends about it. I know this is basic, but don't think because you have finally got your site to the number one spot in Google that your customers are going to love your site—they will just bounce right out of it if it's not what they are looking for.

'Your website is your greatest asset. More people view your webpages than anything else.'

Amanda Sibley
Co-Marketing Manager, HubSpot

A professional SEO service will target this area and develop a specialised SEO campaign that will allow you to both build your brand while proving you customers with a clear next step with how to engage and purchase. This concept brings together many of the areas we have already discussed; link-building, social media, audience profiles. It's all just a matter of tactics and strategy.

Give Your Brand a Voice

When it comes to the online world, it's important that people still recognise you and your business as human. This is one of the best parts of mediums such as social media, but it is especially true when it comes to brand recognition. The general idea is that people want to do business with other people, not with businesses. It's a simple connection to make when you can physically walk into a store down the road and see at a glance the stock, layout, professionalism, and demeanour of the store, but this is harder online.

If you are not too sure what to do here and you don't have $20,000 to invest in an ad agency for them to come up with a great look and feel, then use your own judgement about what websites you like. Whether they are in your industry or not, it will help you to determine what works. Pay attention to what it actually is that you like. I don't care how boring your product or service is, if your website is visually pleasing it will not scare your visitors away. Computers were pretty ugly and boring until Steve Jobs came along. Up to 90% of the buying decision is influenced by design and usability.

I know you're excited about this branding thing Bob, but I haven't seen a car go past all day!

If you focus on humanising your brand, while maintaining professionalism, then it gives your customers a general focus and provides a voice for your business. The three questions you should ask yourself are:

- How well can my customers know me?
- Is my business likeable?
- Is my business considered trustworthy and reliable?

Elements of a Strong Brand

We can all name some of the strong brands that dominate today's markets. They are recognisable for a reason. If you want to grow your brand and have the respect and reputation that you want, then some of the qualities to develop are:

Leadership

The vision that you see for your brand is critical. If you can maintain a strong leadership that gets results and maintains focus then your brand will continue to grow.

Exposure

Your presence is what will be communicating your brand to the world. If you have a regular and positive exposure for your business then it will grow awareness for your brand.

Passion

When times get tough, it is passion that will see your business through to the other side. It is the determination and desire to make a difference that helps to set you apart, and if this is done right, then you can ignite the passion in your customers too.

Audience Knowledge

If you know your audience, you can deliver the results that they want. This means that as your audience may grow and shift, you will always be prepared and maintain professionalism and your brand's worth.

Uniqueness

You need to have your brand be recognisable for what it is. You can't ride the success of another business and demand the same respect. When contemplating this, think about how you best want to be seen, and don't be afraid to be different.

Competitiveness

By knowing what your competitive advantage is, as well as your weaknesses, you can focus upon improvement and maintaining that competitive edge.

Consistency

If you always act with professional consistency then you gain respect through being reliable and upholding a specific standard. A simple solution here is to make sure your website, blog, and social pages all have a branded look and feel. Use consistent colours and images across all platforms.

Strategies in 2016

While a lot of this is simple common sense, there are a few areas that you should pay particular attention to.

Brand Your Content

When generating content you should consider the potential for brand recognition at all times. Ensure it is quality content and the type you want associated with your brand and soon you will start developing the reputation that you want. It's about balancing the need to get your name and brand seen as often as possible, and making sure it is being seen for the right reasons.

Remain Consistent

One of the key areas of brand recognition is consistency and one of the best ways to ensure that you maintain this is to perform regular checks and audits. By having a deliberate look into your actions, you can identify problems, or confirm whether or not you are being consistent. Ask yourself—do your profiles all have the same bio info? Do you have the same visual theme throughout all of your website pages, social media, and correspondence? By maintaining this attention to detail, you can make sure that you are getting credit for everything you do and your brand can be recognised across more areas and platforms.

Google Authorship is Key

If you begin to link your content to a Google+ account then you can directly affect the way that a search result will present your information. This is your Google My Business focus and the result is seeing a short description, an image, and/or google maps results rather than a simple text result. The other benefit to this is that you will have your information under the one heading and this will demonstrate consistency in your image and general brand.

We have discussed at lengths some of the key ways to improve your SEO strategy and get the recognition and visibility you deserve, but sometimes it all goes wrong. The next section will discuss what to do when you discover you have been hit with a penalty.

Charles's Insight

I remember when I first started my online business I was always worried about giving too much information away. I assumed that the best bet was to have potential customers call me so I could explain how amazing our products were on the phone. The only problem with that was that I spent all day on the phone explaining the same eight things to everyone that called.

I then had this simple idea: why don't I put those eight features on my website so I don't have to explain it over and over? It seemed a bit risky, because then my opposition would know what we were doing. I posted those eight FAQs and a few more up on the website, and like magic, the phone calls kept coming in but instead of the average sale taking an additional twenty-five minutes on the phone it took about four minutes. in most cases however they didn't call at all—they just ordered online.

It sounds obvious, but the place to build your online brand is online. Transparency and authenticity is the key to great content. Think of your website like the way you socialise. When you invite your friends around for a dinner, if you spend the whole night making small talk it gets really boring, really quickly. However, if your friends come around for dinner and share their ideas, feelings, and a bit about who they really are, the conversation all of a sudden becomes interesting and meaningful. So it goes with your website; if your website is full of catchy marketing spin and nothing else, your visitors will get bored fast and leave. If you share what is at the heart of your product or service and go into all sorts of details then your visitors will be much more likely to trust you and your brand and buy.

Sharing the best of what you have to offer online in a genuine way will keep your customers coming back for more. If they trust that you are giving them the real story then they will buy. Zig Ziglar put it this way: 'If people like you they'll listen to you, but if they trust you they'll do business with you.'

Be careful about marketing spin, your visitors can sense it a mile away; keep it real and your brand will prosper.

Chapter 11—The Wrath of Google

If you have noticed your rankings in Google have been heading in the wrong direction a possible issue could be Google penalties. This is not unusual and it can be fixed, so don't panic!

Just a word of warning: this chapter is technical—to be honest it's probably not something you as a business owner will do yourself, but it's important you know about these issues. The goal of this chapter is that you learn enough about this subject so you can check in with your SEO team or agency to ensure that you don't have penalties and that you are not using risky strategies that used to work in the past but are no longer a good idea.

Step 1: Do You Have Manual or Algorithmic Penalties?

The first question you need to ask is, is this a manual or an algorithmic penalty? If you have no idea what I'm talking about, talk to your SEO firm or your Webmaster to check this out.

If you suspect that you may be affected by a penalty, then the best way to check is by using Google Webmaster Tools https://www.google.com/webmasters/tools/home?hl=en. After logging in, select 'search traffic' and 'manual actions'. This will display any manual actions that have been taken against you. If there is no notification, then you may need to assume that it is an algorithmic change.

Manual

Manual penalties are the simple ones to identify. You are alerted by a notification through Google Webmaster, where you are told the penalty that is imposed and given various insights into why this has occurred. The types of penalties that you may face vary in severity and depend on whether it is a single page or element, or whether it is your entire domain that is the offending component. You can be slapped with reductions in rankings or even have your domain removed from search engine results. The way you deal with this is by first removing the source of the problem and then submitting a Google 'reconsideration request' (see the final step below).

Algorithmic

Algorithmic penalties are harder to detect and are slower in taking effect. They occur organically as the algorithm used by search engines is changed. The times that this has been most actively felt was when major changes such as Google Penguin and Google Hummingbird were brought into effect. The first indication is a drop in organic traffic numbers. When there is no notification or a manual penalty, but you suspect that something has gone wrong, then it is best to assume that the issue is algorithmic. You should take note of when the issues first began to emerge and then compare that to when updates were released. There are various sites that document the algorithm change history; this is a good place to start.

For the most part though, major algorithmic changes may mean that major work needs to be done to bring your website back in line.

I can't see our website anymore.
I think Google hates us!

While it is impossible to know what is coming next, the best way to try to 'future proof' your SEO strategy is through professional SEO companies that have had experience in adapting to Penguin and Hummingbird. If they are a new business with limited exposure, keep looking. By having experience, they can best optimise your site to the new changes, while having a reasonable expectation of what comes next.

Step 2: Target the Problem

Once you have determined where the problem is coming from you can start to apply a solution and start the recovery process.

Manual

The best place to start is with the penalty notice that Google issued. Its contents should make the problem clear and will list the areas that need attention and rectification. Since Google Penguin, one of the often seen reasons for manual penalties is manipulative link-building. If this is the case, then you are going to need to conduct a link profile audit. You will need to ask, have I bought any links? Are they from poor quality sites? Are the irrelevant? If the answer is yes, then you need to start cutting these links and only then can you start recovering.

Algorithmic

These penalties are harder to address because the cause is not always apparent. The first step is to try to tie the issue to a specific update and then start honing in on a solution. One of the common issues came about when Panda was released; this led to a lot of people auditing the general quality of their site's content, including originality, navigation, and update frequency. These problems are quite often the ones that affect your entire website and will take a longer time to fix, especially when needing to convert to organic links. The most simple and effective way to combat an algorithmic penalty is to consult an SEO firm.

Step 3: Develop a New Strategy

When hit with a penalty, the hardest part is recovering. This is on purpose, as Google wants to deter unethical practices and the results are seen in your subsequent loss of revenue, customer base, and brand recognition. As such, don't take shortcuts, don't engage in unethical practices, and if you don't know what you're doing, approach an SEO firm that doesn't promise anything that is too good to be true.

It is best to be prepared for changes to the algorithm. If you over-deliver in quality content to your audience, then you can be more prepared for any sort of hit to your organic traffic. If you make sure you tick all the boxes and have a strategy that focuses upon the three key features of modern SEO, then you can't fail. Quality content, quality links, and quality social media are the keys to avoiding penalties.

Step 4: Link Audits

If it has occurred to you that bad link methods might be why you are facing these site penalties then the first thing you need to do is conduct a link audit. By conducting an audit you can start to analyse your link profile as a whole and assess the general quality of the links. This auditing process can be anything from a simple informal check, or you may need a professional SEO audit service; many firms will offer this service.

Step 5: Removing Bad Links

When it comes to removing bad links from your site, there are a few different ways to proceed. The first is by trying to physically remove these links or to petition the link owners to have them removed.

This process is known as an outreach campaign and it's important to make sure that you take a systematic approach and document the process. Take note of the following information:

- Site name
- URL of the link
- The anchor text
- URL of the page the link goes to
- Details of the contacts
- Other contact information

The ideal plan is to try to contact the site owners at least three times before you then move onto deciding to discontinue your outreach campaign and resort to other means to remove the bad links. Sometimes you may even come across an especially dishonest site owner who demands payment to remove the link: never pay. Just note down the details in your auditing records and move on. If, after the third attempt to eradicate these bad links, you still haven't heard back or they refuse to remove them, then (and only then) should you turn to Google Disavow.

Step 6: Google Disavow

Google Disavow is an SEO tool that was launched in 2012. The idea is that you use this tool to remove the bad links that are embedded in your site and are stubbornly refusing to leave. This is done by submitting a list of sites that you want removed and Google will then be signalled that you want these links to be ignored. However, this is not a total solution.

It should be clear that you shouldn't need to use it under normal circumstances. This is all reflected in the warnings when engaging the Google Disavow service. This is for two main reasons. Once a link is disavowed, make sure you want it gone. It is a hard process to reinstate any disavowed links. It should only be used after an honest try has been first used to have the unwanted link removed. And secondly, this is an advanced tool so be careful and know what you are doing. There is the potential for this to all go catastrophically wrong if you misuse the disavow tool. If you start with the disavow tool, without giving a good effort at removing these bad links, then it will be looked at negatively by Google down the track.

So to make this clear, start with the good faith actions: start by identifying the sites causing the issue, reach out to them via email to have the links removed, and persist with this action. If you still have no luck, then you can turn to Google Disavow. This does not solve every issue with a bad link and you must always demonstrate caution.

The Final Step: Submitting a Reconsideration Request

Now, once you have realised there is a penalty, have conducted an audit, and removed the bad links, you are ready to get your site operational again. To do this, you will need to submit a Reconsideration Request. Here are a few tips to think about when doing this:

Ensure you have already fixed the problems.

One of the main reasons that a Reconsideration Request will be rejected is that the problem hasn't actually been fixed. Google will not accept a promise to 'get it done soon'. This means that if you have problems with bad links, then remove them first. Be rigorous with your approach; the fact that you have made a more complete and genuine effort to right your wrongs will be favourably considered.

Keep good records.

When facing a manual penalty or submitting a Reconsideration Request, you should be noting everything down in the logs you are keeping. By the end of the process you should aim to have a spreadsheet identifying all the problem areas, the way you have addressed them, and any issues you may have faced. This includes what has been removed, and what was added to Disavow. Be as detailed as possible, because this provides the evidence of your actions and shows that you have made noticeable and genuine changes.

Admit your fault and strive towards a solution.

Ultimately, if you need to submit a Reconsideration Request it's because you have done something wrong or something in contravention of Google's Webmaster policies and as such, you shouldn't try to dodge responsibility. The process will be simpler if you admit fault and demonstrate that you have the solution in place. If you try to shift the blame then Google will be less reluctant to forgive and it will demonstrate that you haven't learnt anything from the experience. Ultimately, they aim to punish people who have done the wrong thing, and it is up to them to decide if you are worthy of a second chance.

The Tactics that Will Always Result in Penalties (Avoid These)

Content spinning, scraping, or duplication.

If your content is stolen from other places, duplicated, or simply poorly written, then it is all a clear indication of a bad site and Google will react accordingly. Original, quality content is what you must aim for.

Buying links.

As made clear in earlier chapters, links are one of the most important and most frustrating elements. Those who cut corners and cheat by buying links will be discovered by Google, and because it violates the Google Webmaster Guidelines, there will be penalties. You need to build quality links, organically and over time.

Links from poor quality sites.

The days of Link Wheels and abused blog links are over and those who continue the practice are subjected to Google penalties. Remove any links that were made dishonestly and you can prevent a Google backlash.

Overuse of anchor text.

When identical anchor text is used or links to your website (and it isn't your site name) then it becomes clear that it is a shortcut job and possibly contains dishonest manoeuvres. To avoid this red flag you need to balance your links through a diverse application of anchor text specified to the environment they are used in.

If you heed this advice then you should avoid violating Google's guidelines and be well-prepared for any algorithmic changes on the horizon.

The next chapter seeks to show you how you can get the best value from your conversion testing and metrics so you get the most out of an SEO campaign.

Charles's Insight

I'm all for being aggressive in your online strategy but for whatever reason, I have never had a penalty on any website. If you have penalties, they can be deadly, so if your current SEO provider has got them, maybe it's time for a change. Penalties will cost you money. Try to get them fixed ASAP and then do as much as you can to ensure they don't occur again.

Chapter 12—Measuring SEO Success—The Power of Measuring Results

Over the years I have spent millions of dollars on sales and marketing campaigns that are really hard to measure. Putting a full-page advert in a leading magazine that costs $40,000 dollars might make you feel special, but knowing exactly how much return you make on that investment is very difficult to measure and, in my experience, is a complete waste of money for most small businesses. The reason I have made millions of dollars from various online businesses over the years is because I have one simple mantra: 'Every marketing cent I spend must directly equate to revenue'. In other words, I don't advertise on buses, billboards, radio, TV; in magazines; or sponsor soccer teams, and the list goes on. I don't care if the whole world knows about my brands or services—I just care about making the maximum amount of revenue for the least amount of marketing cost.

Welcome to the world of SEO. The metrics may, at first glance, seem remarkably boring, but it's all that matters. Figure this stuff out and you will make millions of dollars online.

The joy of online marketing is that you don't spend bucket loads of cash and hope it will pay off.

The Role of Conversions and Metrics in SEO

Performance metrics makes up the information that is gathered that directly informs you of your company's behaviour, performance, and success. Not only does this information help to show you what parts of your strategy are working, but it is crucial in showing your untapped potential and managing your return on investment (ROI).

The reasons should be obvious as to why an analysis of metrics is important to a successful SEO campaign. However, the way in which you collect this information plays a strategic role as well. It's about focusing your efforts in the right areas and not being bogged down with the parts of data that are pointless. You need to start by defining your business goals and then see how this links explicitly to your SEO campaign.

Focus on the Metrics that Matter

When looking at SEO campaigns, you can see that there is a lot of potential for a variety of applications, from developing an audience and increasing traffic to developing effective brand recognition. However, each of these will be focusing upon different elements of metrics.

If you want to develop more affinity with your audience, then the key is to focus on the metrics from social media and newsletter engagement. If, however, your focus is on your return on investment and the bottom line, then your metric focus should be on revenue, repeat customers, substantial purchases, and profits. When faced with hundreds of possible metrics, you need to be able to identify where the relevant information really is and then make sure you can properly interpret what to do with it next. Often digging through this raw data is the hardest part of metrics and it is always a task that an SEO firm will be able to expertly manage.

'To gain insight for more effective content marketing strategy, focus on 3 metrics: performance, operations and ROI.'

Pawan Deshpande
CEO, Curata

Measuring the results from our website
is a snap!

Avoid Vanity Metrics

Sometimes the data that you see can seem interesting and distract you from the important information that will create the insights that you need to succeed. Obsessing about a particular keyword or key phrase in your SEO strategy is a classic example. If you own a sports store that sells Nike cross trainers, don't spend all of your time and money trying to get ranked at number one in Google for 'Nike' or, for that matter, 'Nike Shoes'. No matter what you do, in some cases you will never be the number one site for these keywords because you are not Nike. Google has special SEO exemptions for brand names in their algorithm. These are commonly referred to as 'vanity metrics'. Keep in mind at all times that your focus for any business should be:

- **Customers:** leads, subscriptions, repeat purchase actions
- **Revenue:** Sales, profits, value, customers, large actions sales
- **Conversions:** the key areas that drive people to take action, or conversely, what is detracting from this

Outside of these areas, keep an eye out for any sort of metrics that yield information about short-term results, or those that answer any specific questions that you may have. These areas are important because they can help to inform your decision-making process and provide you with short-term feedback and reaffirm the direction you are taking.

If you are looking outside of these three areas, then chances are, your time could be better spent elsewhere.

'Traditional ROI measures are flawed. Focus on measuring content vs. teams, both quality and quantity, and see ROI as progress, not a destination.'

Robert Rose
Chief Strategy Officer, Content Marketing Institute

Conversion Testing: Showing You What Actually Works

Conversion testing is a fundamental area for SEO analysis as it indicates the level of traffic you receive versus the number that actually engage with your site. The focus of SEO is to push your site into using the best value strategies, in using a variety of tactics to improve your organic search results, however if you are succeeding here, but not actually converting this interest into sales, then you are ultimately wasting your time.

Conversion testing is a way to understand which elements of your marketing and SEO strategy are actually working for you, and which ones are not. Through conversion testing, information about what sort of areas drew success will be focused upon. For instance, if during one month the release of a product through one avenue led to 10% sales, but through another produced 25%, then the second will be naturally viewed more favourably. This is all part of a systematic marketing approach that is engaged through a professional SEO firm. They can test different approaches with your business to measure the results that come back and then start showing you which paths to take, and which parts to stop investing time and energy into.

Our last chapter will run through a few of the best tools and resources for SEO and how they can apply to all of the areas that we have discussed.

Charles's Insight

Over the years I have gone through all sorts of phases when it comes to the metrics that measure a particular website's performance. The data is important; in fact, it's critical. Split-testing campaigns or even websites are also important. There is, however, one metric that trumps all others when it comes to measuring your website's success and that is whether you are actually making money or not. I know it sounds obvious, but sometimes it's not your online strategy that is failing—it's your product or service, your sales process, or your business model.

The best SEO in the world can't fix that. A simple AdWords campaign can help you in this process. For example, let's take Bob and Sue. They have a wonderful health retreat in the mountains and the point of their website is to have people spend a weekend or week at their retreat. A very brief AdWords campaign will be able to shortcut years of wasted SEO effort. They will learn two simple things in those two weeks that will shape their SEO strategy for a long time to come.

1. They learn the keyword phrase that matters the most for them is 'Weekend Health Retreats'.
2. They learn that the ad that worked best from the range of ads they used was 'Special Offer—Weekend Retreat from $195 call 1300 421 435'.

From just looking at this simple data, they learn so much about what appeals to their potential customers. From the keywords they know what to focus on. From the Display Ad in AdWords they know a simple call to action on the home page with the words 'special offer' and a price is powerful with their audience.

They change their home page to reflect that sort of feedback and in two short weeks they are already on their way to having their website make money. They gave up some of their design ideas on the home page to make way for a simple call to action, and all of a sudden bookings started rolling in. Remember that most people, even if they buy from your site, don't have much time. Don't make people look for how to order from your site; it will cost you.

This simple example shows how measuring what is happening is so powerful for you as a website owner. Don't only focus on traffic; traffic won't pay the bills. Focus on making sales.

If you need more information about your own SEO strategy or need some friendly advice, feel free to visit my website: www.slingshotinternetmarketing.com.

Section II
Start Making Money Online

Chapter 13—Seven Rules to Start-up Success

There are seven important rules to follow if you want to build an online lifestyle business

Rule No. 1—Start Small

One of the things the internet has radically changed over the past twenty years is our ability to get into business for little to no cost. When I was in my early twenties I was fortunate enough to work for a very large company in a fantastic role, and it had all the trimmings of a great job. It had the flexible hours, great salary, expense account, nice office full of nice people—the lot. To be successful in the role wasn't particularly difficult, so life was good. I was newly married, starting a small family, and building our first home. There was only one problem with the job; I hated it! It was soul destroying—the politics, the jargon, the 'keep your head down and don't rock the boat' mentality. I was convinced I could do a far better job of running the business than the current management. (Remember I was twenty-three.)

So, not really having any idea what I could or should do, I decided to dip my toe into an idea that I had. Before I quit my nice job I would start my new business on the side, in my lunch break. I had no money so I was forced to start small. Initially I spent about $100, printed up some business cards, and while I was on my lunch break from my full-time job I walked door-to-door selling my product. After about three months of that I had made enough money to spend about $15,000 dollars on some equipment that would help me to no longer buy my product from a supplier, as I could produce the product in-house. This equipment allowed me to lower my costs as well as to control my delivery times. After making that decision I then quit my corporate career, never to return. This small business grew over the years and started me out on the road of self-employment. At the time $15,000 was a huge amount of money to risk, but it wasn't so scary because I already had some clients and revenue.

There is nothing remarkable about this story and you hear them all the time, but I want to use it as an example of a strategy that I still feel strongly about. I have started forty+ businesses since that first one and I have always followed the same principles because I have a problem with losing money on a bad idea.

Rule No. 2—Only Invest What You Can Afford to Lose

When I was twenty-three I had $100 I could afford to lose. Any more than that would have been too much. I was happy to throw the business cards away and write the idea off as a lesson learned and that would be that. I was happy to use my lunch breaks and other spare time to see if my idea would fly.

I call this the 'casino rule': if you want to enjoy your time in a casino and gamble away some of your hard-earned cash then you need to follow this one simple rule so it will be fun and not a terrible experience. Walk into the casino with a designated amount of cash you are happy to lose, let's say $20. Then start on very small gambles, on the five and ten cent machines, to build up your reserves and then take any winnings you can. Do not risk any win with the temptation of the double or nothing option; take any win no matter how small. Once you have back your original $20, put it in your pocket and leave it there; that's for the cab home. Then gamble with the profits. Once they have gone or you're bored, go home. Please note, I do not gamble and in no way do I think it's a good idea, nor do I want you to take my gambling advice as literal—it's just a story.

I share these two seemingly unrelated stories to illustrate the same point. The entrepreneur/small business owner's journey is really hard and you will make mistakes. I could write a very big book about all my mistakes. I know what it's like to make money and go broke. I have learned some things along the way that ensure I mitigate as much risk in every business decision as possible. Don't invest more into your idea than you are prepared to lose. For example, if you have a great business idea that requires you to borrow $100,000 dollars, make sure you have that cash in reserve somewhere so if it goes to custard then you pay the debt and move onto another idea.

When your business can afford to pay you back, then do it. Invest your profits in growing the business. If you can afford to build a basic website to see how things go then that's all you do. If you can afford to run a PPC/AdWords campaign for a month to see how things go then do that, just set a figure in stone and don't chase the losses. Casinos make all their money from gamblers chasing their losses. They lose $1000 so they spend another $5,000 trying to win back the $1000.

Rule No. 3—Keep Your Current Cash Flow

If you remember, I didn't quit my job to figure out if the idea was any good. This one is important; most small businesses fail in the first twelve months. Statistically it's very likely you will have some false starts, so keep whatever you do for an income now so you can eat and keep a roof over your head. An online business is perfect because you can work on it after hours and in your spare time. If your idea is rubbish then you will find out soon enough.

Rule No. 4—Don't Take Failure Personally

That first business I started had far more failures than victories. I made so many classic mistakes in that business, which kept me scraping by for years. I could have assumed that I was not cut out for the job of running a small business, but instead I kept trying different things and other business ideas. All the mistakes, all 500 of them, that I made with that first business I didn't make again with the next business I started. In the next business I made about 200 more. So in the next business again, I didn't make the first 700 mistakes and my ability to make money improved accordingly.

'Failures are part of life. If you don't fail, you don't learn.
If you don't learn, you'll never change.'

Anon

When it comes to your online strategy, you will make mistakes, experimenting with different ideas and finding out what works. One trap I think many start-up entrepreneurs make is that they assume failure means they are not built to do the job. Entrepreneurship, much like anything else, is something you need to learn. If I thought you could do a weekend seminar to make millions and it was that simple I'd suggest you put this book in the bin and go and do it. However it's not really like that; you still have to go on the journey and put in the hard yards.

'We pay a heavy price for our fear of failure. It is a powerful obstacle to growth. It assures the progressive narrowing of the personality and prevents exploration and experimentation. There is no learning without some difficulty and fumbling. If you want to keep on learning, you must keep on risking failure all your life.'

John W. Gardner

I remember as a young father wondering if I had done the right thing to have kids in my early twenties. I used to think to myself that maybe if I had waited until I was more established in my life, until I wasn't building my first house, wasn't trying to battle through the poverty of full-time study, wasn't constantly borrowing the neighbour's mower because I couldn't afford my own, or starting my own business—I would have found being a dad a much easier gig. Until one day I was chatting with a client, who happened to be a very successful lawyer in his late thirties, and he was excitedly telling me that he and his wife were having their first child. I congratulated him and thought to myself, wow, it's going to be much easier for that guy to spend time with his family because he is so established in his career and financial status.

About four years later I met up with this client again. He was looking pretty tired and four years older, of course. We got to chatting about things and I asked about his family and they had since had another baby so the family had grown to include two children. I asked how family life was and he was positive and happy about family life. He explained many of the challenges associated with having small children in the house and the hectic lifestyle that happens as a result. He was complaining about the lack of sleep and a few other things that I resonated with because I had been through it also, like all parents. Then the thought occurred to me; it doesn't matter what you know or what stage of life you are at, the lessons you need to learn raising young children are the same for everyone. There is no ideal preparation, no handbook, no time-out, no change in your way of thinking. For all of us, we learn by experience and by doing; there are just some things we need to experience to learn.

Much like parenting, much of what we need to learn as an entrepreneur is not going to be learned with an MBA or a spreadsheet; it's going to be learned by having a crack at it.

Rule No. 5—You Know Enough

I know wonderful academics who can teach wonderful business classes at university. They know far more than I do about the global economy but couldn't run a chook raffle, because many of the most important lessons you will learn in a small online business are learned by application or by going through the process, like I mentioned in my previous rule.

Albert Einstein said this about reading, but I apply it to studying or reading too much into the theory of running a business:

> *Reading, after a certain age, diverts the mind too much from its creative pursuits. Any man who reads too much and uses his own brain too little falls into lazy habits of thinking.*

Please don't misunderstand this rule; I'm not saying blindly jump on board with any half-brained idea you and your friends come up with around the BBQ after a few stiff drinks. What I'm saying is, be careful not to dismiss your own experience and creativity as insufficient when it comes to starting an online business. You don't have to be a world leading expert to be successful. You don't have to have an MBA. You have all that it takes. You don't even have to have a nice car or have been a CEO of a global organisation. You probably already have what it takes to build a website and have a go.

I have a friend who was the president of a very large global organisation with over 25,000 staff worldwide. He was paid a ridiculous amount of money, and was highly qualified and a very smooth operator. He was intelligent and good with people. By the age of fifty he had basically achieved everything you could achieve in the corporate world. The day came when he was replaced as the CEO and he found himself out of a job. After about a year of being over-qualified for almost every job he applied for he decided to go into business with his son, who was a dry-cleaner. They decided to buy a local dry-cleaning business ten minutes from their house. It seemed like the perfect arrangement; with Dad's amazing resume and the son's technical skills, what could go wrong? I remember thinking, wow, imagine applying all of my friend's corporate experience to a humble dry-cleaning business, this will be amazing.

The previous owners weren't making any money so they almost gave the business away, so my friend and his son and some other family members all got into this new venture with all the enthusiasm that you do when you are taking on a new family business.

It wasn't too long before I heard my highly qualified friend tell me some of the challenges with the business. About a year later my friend sold the business for the exact same amount they bought it for the year before. It nearly destroyed their family and their sanity. My friend complains there isn't too much you can do in that sort of business; you're stuck in your location, totally dependent upon walk-by traffic, etc. I remember thinking at the time—and I still think this way—that maybe the skills to run a large global organisation are completely different to those needed for a small start-up business. Either way, the point of the story is that I'm sure if you are starting an online business you are nowhere near as qualified as my friend was and he still couldn't make it happen. So don't wait until you know everything before you start to live your dreams, because if you do you will never start.

Rule No. 6—Good Economics

Imagine for a minute you could dream up the perfect online business. What would it look like? If you can't imagine one, think of a great website or online business. What makes it amazing? Some of the most amazing online businesses are cash cows—not because they have come up with some amazing new creative idea, but because the model is right. I will give you a few examples of what I mean. Imagine if you were sitting around the table when someone suggested selling books online as a multi-million dollar website. I wonder how that meeting would have gone?

Your idea doesn't have to be amazingly new or radically creative; it just has to have good economics. Warren Buffet put it this way: 'When management with a reputation for brilliance tackles a business with a reputation for bad economics, it is the reputation of the business that remains intact.' Let me give you my guaranteed, sure-fire rule that will ensure your online business isn't just buying you a job, but generating wealth. Make sure the economics of your business model are right. Let me put it another way. If you are a talented gardener and you love mowing lawns, trimming trees, etc. Let's suppose you are pretty busy and you charge $40 per hour; you enjoy working on your own with no staff or headaches. Then one weekend a friend at a BBQ suggests you build a website and do some SEO so you can get more customers. You think to yourself, *That's a great idea, I really should have a website; it's what everyone expects these days*. So you Google an SEO company and off you go. Sure enough, after a while you start to get some customers from your website. You are happy about it; you have some more work to do. The problem is that you soon realise that no matter how many new customers you get, you can only work so many hours in the day and $40 per hour is the maximum you can make.

Now blind Freddy can see what the problem here is with the gardener's business model. He has essentially bought himself a job. Now please understand, if you are sitting there feeling offended because you are happy with your $40 per hour, then put this book down—don't read on, because it's about to get pretty ugly. If you want to build wealth online, the economics have to work first and foremost. You may be in an industry—

and there are plenty of them—that has an hourly rate culture, and that's fine, just don't expect to make any real money if it's just you doing the work for that hourly rate.

Some of you may be thinking that the solution to that gardener's problem is just to get more staff, pay them $30 per hour, and make $10 per hour profit. In some cases that may be the simple answer, but in most cases, the headaches and the stress of paying employee gardeners' wages on the rainy days can send you broke pretty quickly. Either way, that is not what I'm talking about.

Here is what I mean by good economics: whenever you personally need to work for one hour to earn one hour's pay, then your economics are bad. Unless of course you can charge $20,000 per hour, it's bad. If you want to build wealth and make millions of dollars and still have a great life, you need to avoid that model. If you are just looking to make wages or a bit better, then go for it.

The gardener, for example, instead of building a website that helps him find more customers, would be better served building a website for the industry he is in. He could build a gardening exchange where people who need gardeners can go onto the website and order a gardener. All the gardeners that want extra work pay an annual membership and get the extra work in their area. I haven't spent five seconds thinking about this idea; it's probably already being done all over the world, in all sorts of cities, but the point is that this website will make money day and night and especially on the wet days. This website will make our gardener friend some passive income and start him on his way to building real wealth.

Rule No. 7—Beware of the Start-up Traps

Business plans? If you are looking to raise capital for a new start-up then I suggest you have a rock solid business plan. But in the context of a low cost, debt-free start-up, the best business plan will be making sales. You could spend six months developing an almighty business plan that would impress your most intelligent friends, but when you implement the plan it goes nowhere. In some respects a business plan is just a well-documented idea. I have a good friend who has given me at least 300 good business ideas over the years and he is still broke. A good idea/business plan is a great intellectual exercise in the low cost start-up model, but will keep you broke; build a website and make some sales, save yourself six months of your life.

Lipstick on the Pig

Don't waste what little start-up money you have with an expensive ad agency creating a great look and feel with logos, brochures, videos, and websites before you have sold a thing. It's natural to want to make your products or services present as well as possible, but in most cases you might just be putting lipstick on that pig. No matter how much you put on, it's still a pig. Spend your start-up money on getting your product to market as cheaply as you can, then once you have it making you money, use your profits to re-brand and get an amazing look.

Financial Commitments

Online businesses are normally free from things like rental leases on shop fronts and staff. In both of these cases the business involves a substantial commitment. For a shopfront in a shopping mall it can be up to a minimum of five year lease. With staff, hiring is easy, but depending on where you live, firing is not so easy. Start with you and family so if your online business doesn't fly it's easier to walk away. If you are looking for a lifestyle business then staff usually need management, and unless you get to a certain size very quickly, guess who will be doing the management until then?

Avoid Partners

I'm not talking about a joint venture here, I'm talking about a partnership agreement. This is a great way to lose friends and create headaches. It's hard enough having a relationship with your spouse whom you love and share children with, let alone making a go of a business partnership. If you are looking for a lifestyle online business to build wealth, then a partner will not be a good option. You will either work harder or not as hard as your partner. You will have a different idea about how to invest profits, you will want to take some profit for a holiday and your partner won't like holidays. You will always get to the office two hours earlier than your partner. Your partner will spend an hour on Facebook when everyone else is working at a frantic pace. Your partner won't want to take any risks, stifling the growth of your business. Your partner will want to have three months off when his wife has a baby. Your partner will hate the way you treat your staff. Are you getting the idea? Sometimes you may be chatting to a friend and collectively come up with a great idea, so you both start saying 'Hey, why don't we use this great idea for a website,' etc. At that point you say, 'I would like to continue to be your friend, so you go and do that idea, I'm too busy at the moment.' It will seem like the best idea in the world at the beginning but it will be all downhill from there. Now I'm not saying partners can't work; there is plenty of evidence around to demonstrate they can. I'm talking about an online lifestyle business, where you work when and how you want. If you have a partner, you will feel guilty for taking the afternoon off to laze around your pool reading a book. If your lifestyle business (or a partner) won't let you do that, then you don't have a lifestyle business.

Chapter 14—AdWords is Your Friend—Test Your Model

This chapter could save you thousands of wasted SEO dollars. Warning—do not start a new website or online business SEO campaign without an AdWords campaign first. The reason is very simple: you could spend twelve months ranking where you want organically with the keywords you need, only to find out you have spent thousands of dollars on an idea that just doesn't work. In other words, this process allows you to test your business model. AdWords will be the quickest and most inexpensive way to see if your online idea or business will actually make you money. Once you know it will take off and make you money, then and only then can you start spending on a good SEO campaign.

You can establish whether or not your online strategy will work without spending thousands on an agency. Simply follow the steps below and I will guide you through the process of starting an AdWords campaign and finding keywords.

My passion for years has been internet marketing and, more specifically, SEO. One of the reasons I grew a passion for it was because I knew I didn't want to be enslaved to Google for the rest of my life, paying for AdWords to send visitors to my websites. For some of my websites I have paid up to $30 per click or visitor to my website, and at that rate you can go broke really fast.

The reason you want to be actively doing SEO for your website is to eliminate that cost. If you can have a website organically getting twenty visits a day that would normally cost you $30 per visit, then you are saving $600 a day on an AdWords campaign. Sounds basic, right?

The reason AdWords is your friend is because it will allow you to test your business idea or website in the real world. Let's take Bob and Sue for example: they run their health retreat and now they have decided to create a new website selling yoga products. Because they know their stuff, they have all the good connections, they know the right equipment to buy, they have the best clothing, they have mats, etc. Bob gets his SEO/web design company to whip him up a pretty basic site. He doesn't want to spend too much because he knows my rules about starting up a business. Bob and Sue are not sure if the website will actually make any money, so instead of spending thousands of dollars creating an amazing SEO campaign, they simply decide to run a two-week trial with AdWords to see how things will go first.

It is absolutely useless driving traffic to their site with a slick SEO strategy if they don't make sales once the visitors arrive. There is no quicker way to test your online strategy than a few weeks running a Google AdWords campaign. Set a budget that you can afford to lose in case nothing comes of it, and see how you go. If it turns a profit, then you may want to consider a good, long-term SEO strategy. But if at the end of two weeks all you got were expensive visitors, then something is wrong and you need to make changes.

As an entrepreneur you need to have some understanding of how you can educate yourself online. The idea is that this book will give you enough of an understanding to at least manage your SEO strategy in a productive way. But before you take that step and find a good internet marketing company, dabble with a couple of the Google tools yourself so you can get a feel for the potential traffic and visitors you could get to your site.

The first tool before you set up an AdWords campaign that is really essential, is that you have an understanding the Google Keyword Planning Tool.

Google AdWords

Depending on where you are in the process of online marketing, chances are you have heard of Google AdWords.

It's one of the simplest and most popular ways to advertise within the Google search engine. The results are seen on any Google Search—the first few results, or the results to the right of your page with the yellow 'ads' signs, are all paid ads through Google AdWords.

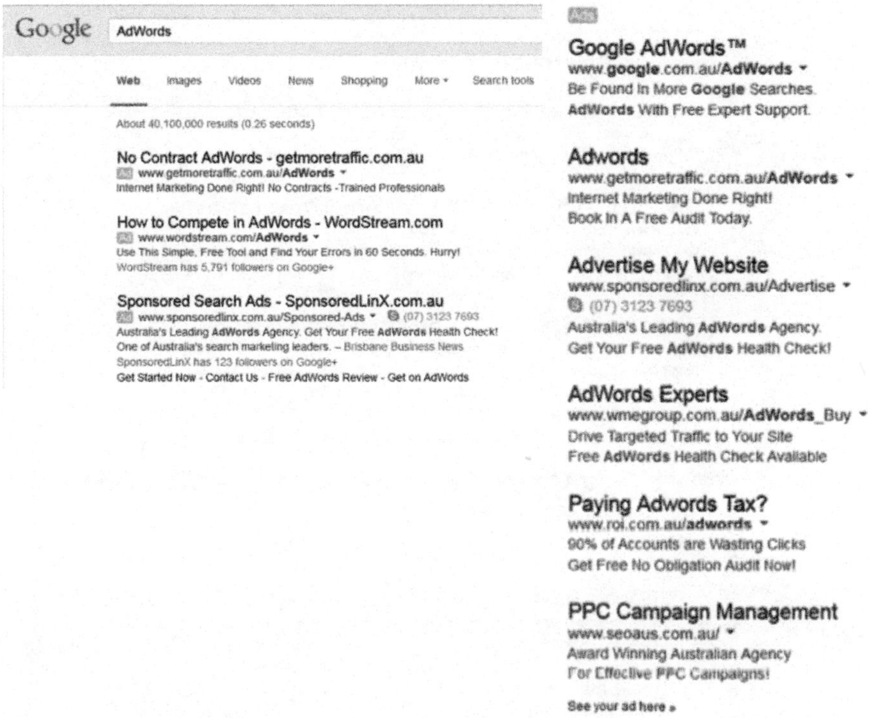

Creating an Account and Your First Campaign

The first step to creating your Google AdWords account is to access the website at https://www.google.com.au/adwords/ or simply search for 'AdWords' and click on the appropriate result (underneath the ads).

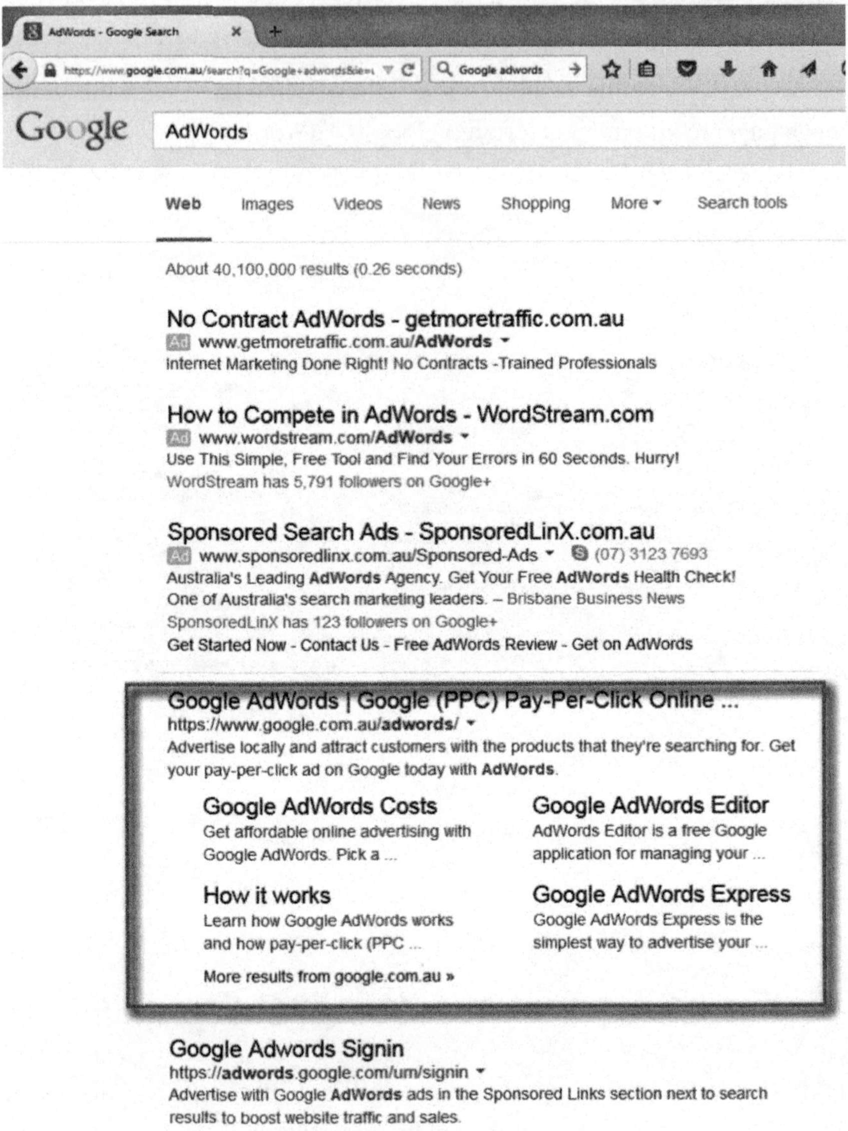

The Google AdWords home page is a simple gateway page where you can find out further information, contact them if needed, or simply get started straight away.

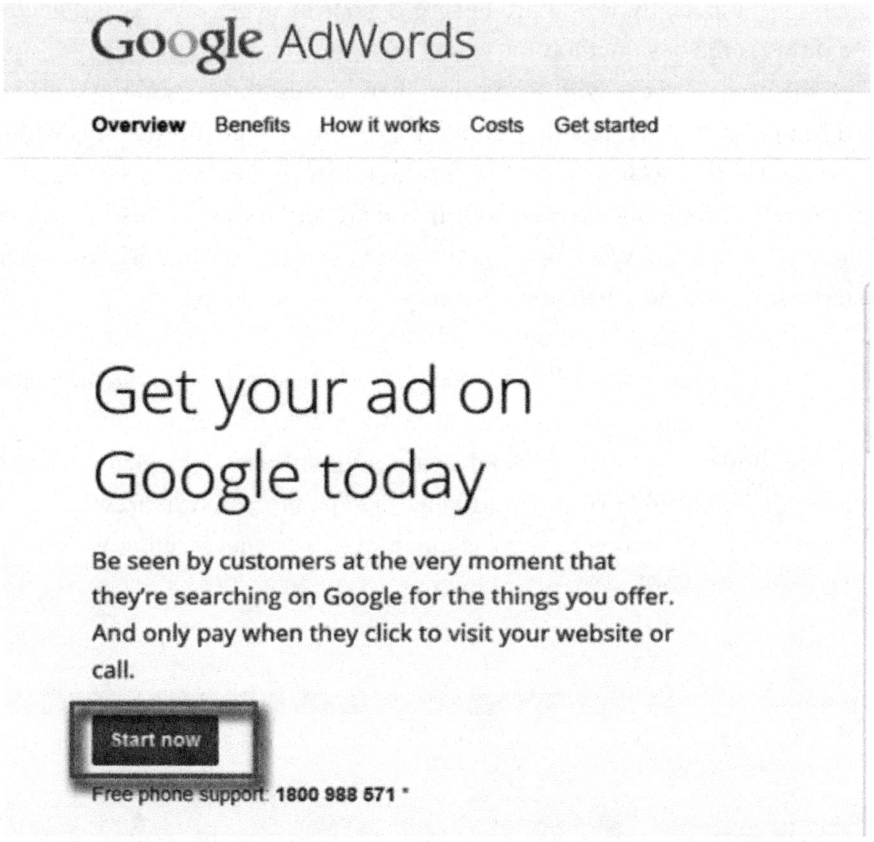

Additional information about the process can be found under the tabs along the top:

- Overview
- Benefits
- How it works
- Costs
- Get started

But the important thing to note throughout the process is that there are no upfront costs, no commitments, and no obligations to actually create an ad and have it displayed. Signing up for AdWords can seem a little daunting, especially if you are unsure if your business advertising needs, or if this is the best method for you.

The process starts with the basics, then moves on to creating your first ad campaign, billing, and then a review. You need to go through this whole process in order to fully create an account. Which means yes, you need to enter your billing information. But if you are still unsure if this is for you, the very first thing you can do is disable your first ad campaign and then start with a new ad when you are ready.

Once ready, click on 'Start Now'.

Once you have started the process, the first step is to enter the email address you want to use to manage the account. Any email address will suffice, however we recommend using a Gmail account because it will save you the trouble of having to link a separate email address. This is because Google prefers to keep as much of its systems together whether it is Google, AdWords, Gmail or Google+.

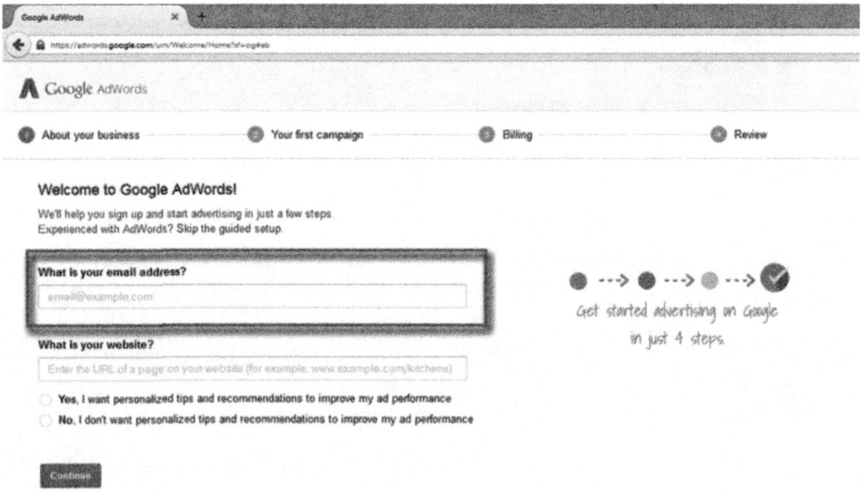

Once you have entered your email address, you next need to link your website. For this, simply enter the home page URL. And feel free to either tick yes or no in the recommendations box.

When done, click 'Continue' and you will start planning your first campaign.

At the top of the next page, chances are that you will see the following banner:

This simply gives you the choice of using AdWords or AdWords Express to manage your first campaign. AdWords Express is a scaled down version that was originally known as Google Boost.

It's a feature aimed at reducing the difficulty of managing the ad by automatically approaching areas such as managing keywords and ad placement. This is created with small businesses in mind. If you find that Google AdWords has decided not to recommend AdWords Express, or if you simply want to use the normal AdWords, then feel free.

Don't worry, you aren't locked in to one system or the other. At the end of the process you can choose to disable your AdWords Express campaign and replicate it in traditional AdWords.

I find it simpler to use AdWords Express for new people, and as such I will take you through the process now.

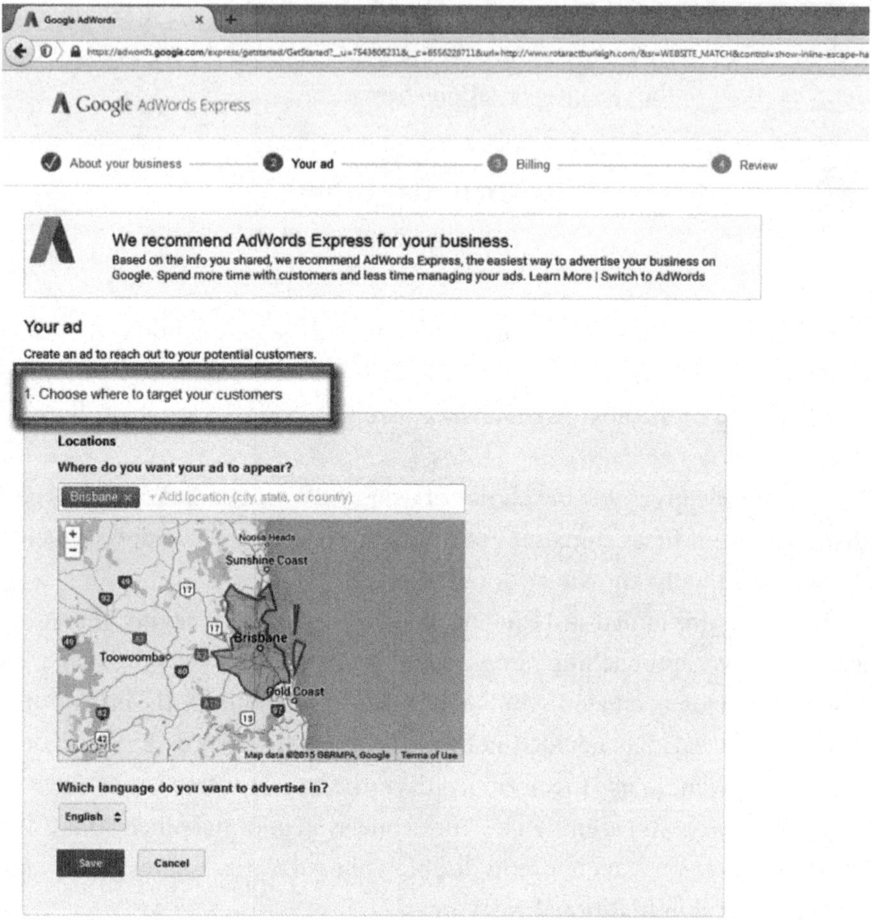

You now get to start planning your first ad, first step—location.

For the location, simply add in all the relevant locations that you want your ad to target. If you are local to Brisbane, then consider adding places in the surrounding areas, or if you are a national business, then feel free to enter 'Australia'. This step all depends on the nature of your business and who your targeted audience is. You also have the option here to choose what language you advertise in.

When ready, click 'Save' and move onto the next step.

Step 2 is selecting the nature of your advertisement.

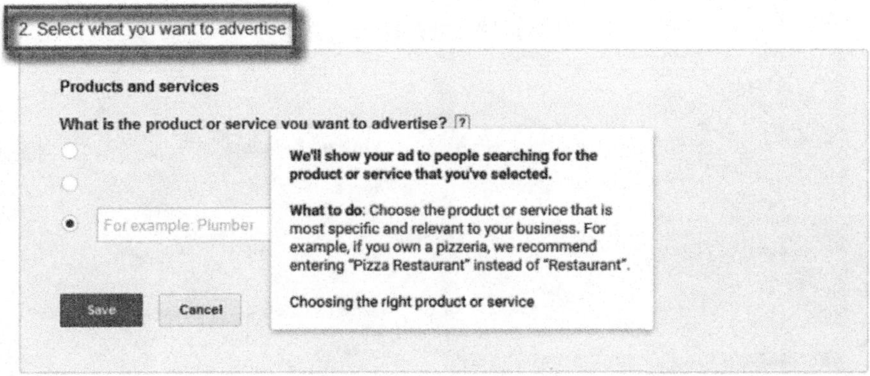

For this, enter in what your business is and AdWords will then prompt you with further subdivisions of that role, which you can tick or untick. This process helps to narrow down the keywords that you want your ad to appear for. It is a more complicated process outside of AdWords Express, but there are also some rather helpful tools here to help you through it. For now, select what is most appropriate for your business and select 'Save'.

Step 3 is writing your ad.

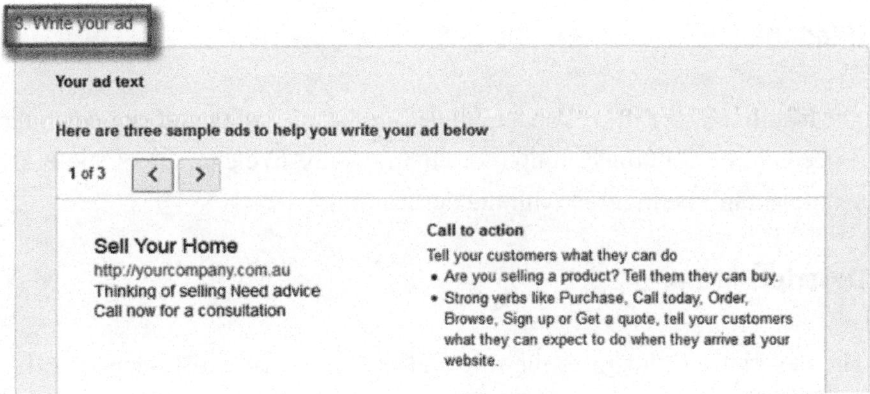

AdWords Express helps you out here by providing you with a few examples, as well as showing you a preview of what the ad will look like.

Keep in mind that there are a limited number of characters per line, as shown in the grey numbers to the right of each section.

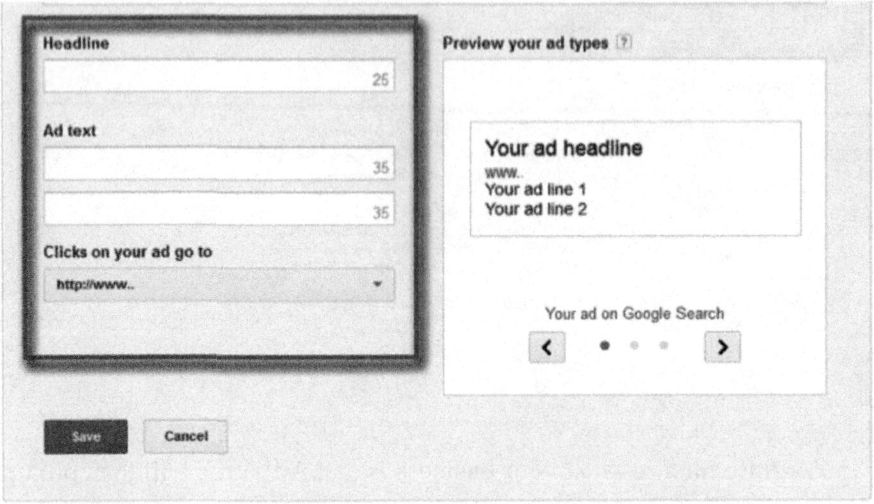

Ad copy should also be written in the local language and be free from spelling mistakes, typos, and grammar errors.

Your First Ad

Headline

The headline is the title of an ad. It needs to be appealing and eye-catching! It needs to be contained in no more than twenty-five characters. Note: the headline can't be merged with the descriptions.

Description 1 and 2

The description illustrates the title and offers a great call-to-action (CTA) to incite the reader to click on the ad. Please note that the two lines can either be composed of two parts of a sentence or two small sentences. It can be read at one time. So you can start a sentence in the description 1 and finish it in the description 2—that's absolutely fine. Each description line can not exceed thirty-five characters.

Display URL

It is the URL displayed on the ad but it could be different from the actual one if it is too long or too complicated. A display URL can contain the keyword or the search intent in the URL path to be more relevant.

Official Rules for Writing Ads

- Only one exclamation mark, and no exclamation mark in the headline
- Do not use the word 'click' or anything that is inconsistent with the presentation of Google searches as per their policy
- No abusing of upper case
- Respect the character limits

All the rules for Google ads are detailed here: https://support.google.com/adwordspolicy/answer/176095?hl=en-G/B

The preview also shows you how your ad will look on traditional searches as well as on mobile searches and for other engines so you can appreciate how your ad will look for all options. Once you are happy, click 'Save'.

The last step for your ad is selecting your budget.

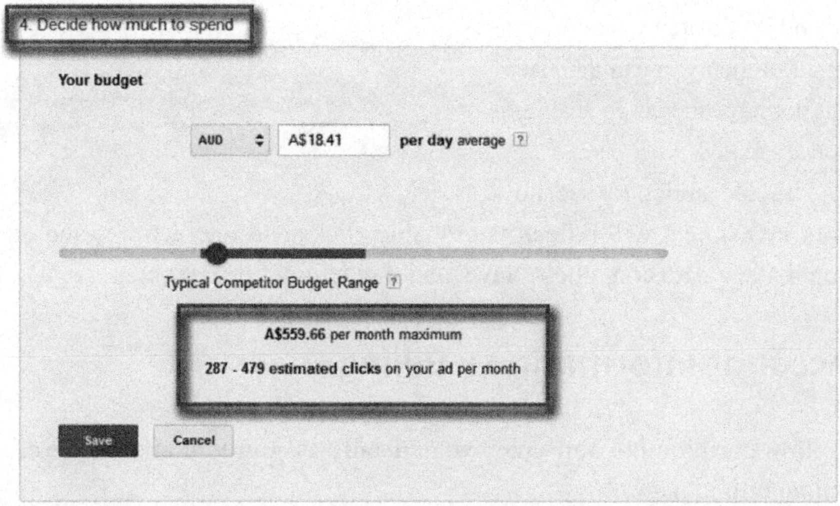

Google AdWords Express has a useful slider tool that shows you roughly how your costs can translate into clicks on the ad.

As they state on the home page, it's a 'no visit, no fee' system. The way it works is based upon a bidding system, which means that the cost of your ad may change on a day-to-day basis based on its popularity. This bidding is done automatically and you will always be charged the lowest possible amount. This is why you set your daily and monthly budget—so that your possible total bids will never exceed the amount that you are comfortable paying.

The slider also has a darker section to indicate the typical range where people in your industry usually select their budget. Keep this in mind when choosing your budget because you need to make sure that you find a price that you are comfortable with that remains competitive in your chosen market.

Don't be too worried about this step though—as we mentioned before, if you are still unsure of the process, feel free to just create a generic ad to see how it works. When you get through to the dashboard at the end you can disable your ad and start fresh when you have a greater understanding of what you want. It is unfortunate that to sign up you need to step through this 'first ad' creation process, but you are never locked into this ad and if you aren't sure of what to select then you can take steps but not have the ad go live until you are ready.

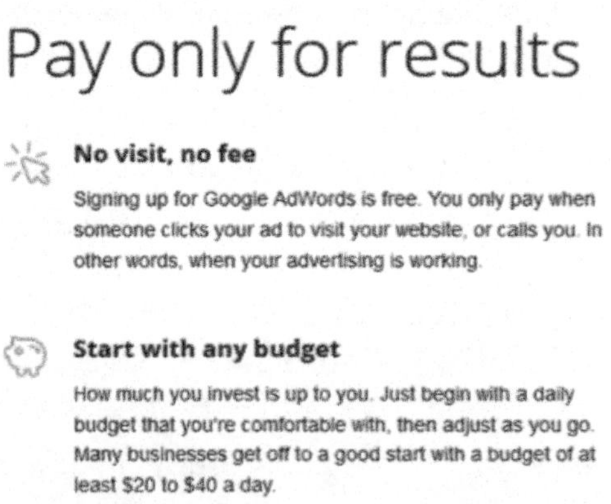

Use the slider to see how your investment will reflect its probable clicks and interactions, and once you make a decision, click 'Save' and move on to the next step.

Account Information—Billing

Follow the prompts and enter your details as you would for any other online billing page.

Keep in mind that Google AdWords does not charge anything to you unless your ad is active and generating traffic. This process is simply a way to get your card on file, so if you select your ad to go active then these are the banking details to be charged.

Once you are done here, you get to review your ad one last time before finalising your AdWords Account. Then you are done—you have created an AdWords account and your first ad.

Now that you have created your Google AdWords account through Express, you should find yourself at the homepage for AdWords Express.

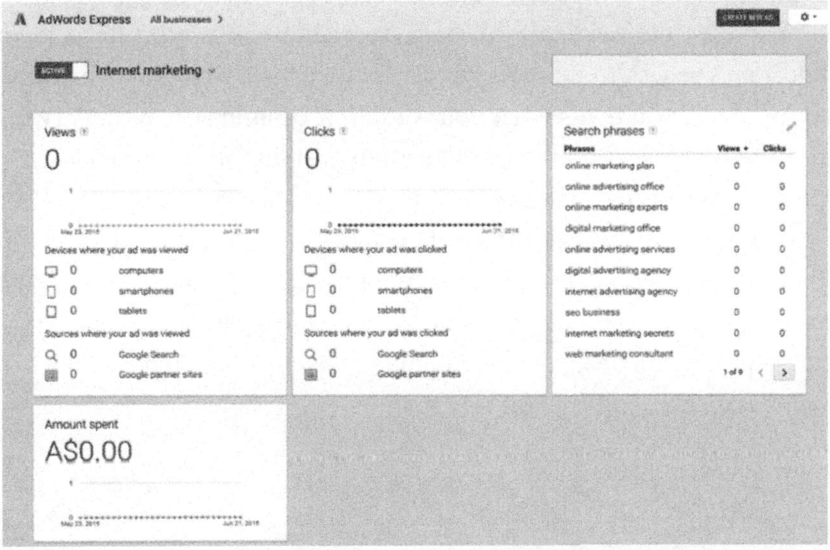

As we mentioned, if you aren't happy to go ahead with the ad you created, you can very easily disable your service and you won't be charged anything until you are ready to go ahead.

To do this, simply click on the 'Active/Inactive' button, follow the prompts, and answer (or don't) the brief response.

Again, Google AdWords has both a regular version and an express version. The express version is a stripped down and simplified management tool which lets you create new campaigns but doesn't have the tools for keyword research and gives you only limited interaction in some areas.

The important thing to note is that if you create a campaign through AdWords Express, you can only manage it through AdWords Express; they are all still the same account, but just need to be accessed through their respective areas.

Above we have stepped you through Google AdWords Express because it is a slimmed down account and a first campaign system that is easier to grasp.

We prefer the original AdWords version because you have greater control and access to your Keyword Tools, which we will be discussing later on. So if you realise that you want to predominantly used AdWords, not AdWords Express, you can quite easily just disable your campaign and replicate it in the traditional AdWords.

We will now take you through your dashboard. Google Express is rather simple: you have your ad summary page, and then your business page; from the home page you can manage multiple businesses and ads, and by clicking on one, you are brought to the info about that business—its results, statistics, and general information if you want to make changes.

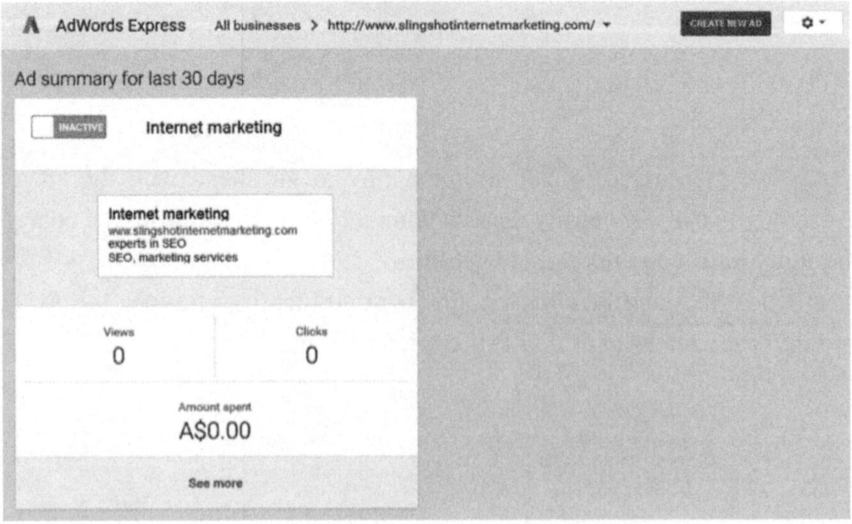

This is the ad summary page. If you click on 'See more' you are brought to the page you landed on earlier, with the data regarding this ad.

If you want to create a new ad you follow these steps:

1.) Click on the big orange button stating 'Create New Ad'
2.) Follow the prompts as per your first campaign above

As you can see, Google AdWords Express is exactly as promised. It's simple and straightforward to use. Google AdWords works in much the same way as AdWords Express; we will take you through this process now.

Because you have now created your AdWords account, when you go to access the system the default page is the traditional AdWords, but you also have the option of accessing AdWords Express. Keep in mind that as mentioned earlier, these two systems use the same account, but run separate campaigns. On your AdWords dashboard, you may notice a notification in the top right corner.

This means that you need to make sure you manage both system's ads, or alternately choose one or the other exclusively.

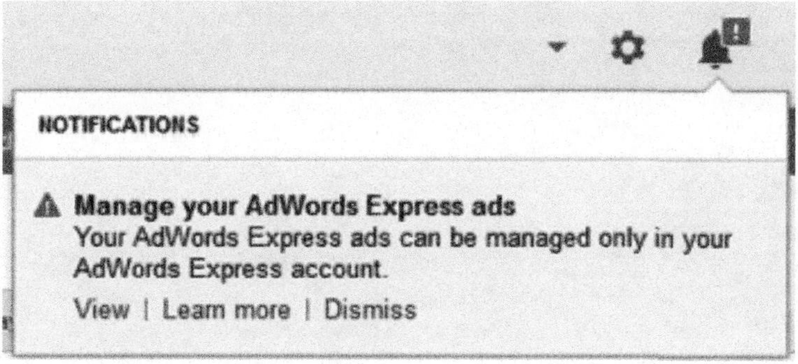

The AdWords homepage provides you with a greater overview of all of your campaigns and their results.

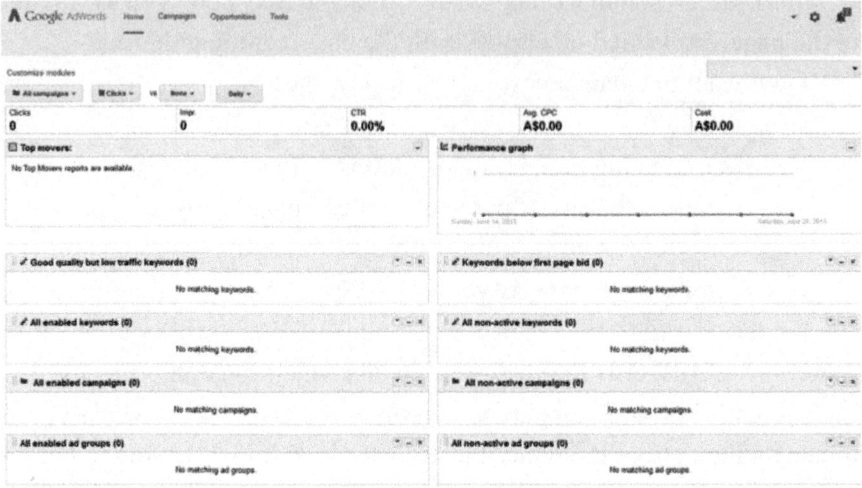

Here, as you can see, we have no campaigns running, but these can be created and managed from the 'Campaigns' tab.

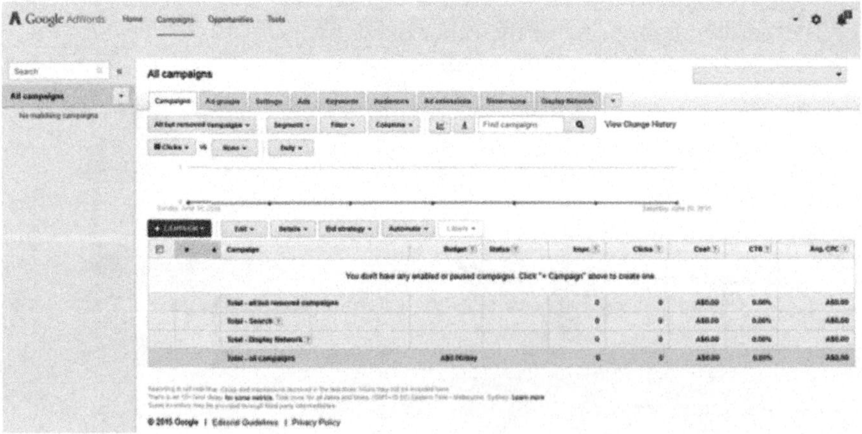

The Campaigns tab allows you to create and manage your ad campaigns. From here you can create a new campaign by selecting the 'Campaign' button.

When talking about campaigns, it is important to know a bit about the structure of AdWords and how all of your keywords, ads, and campaigns come together.

Within your new account you can create a series of campaigns; consider each one as a separate idea or target within your business.

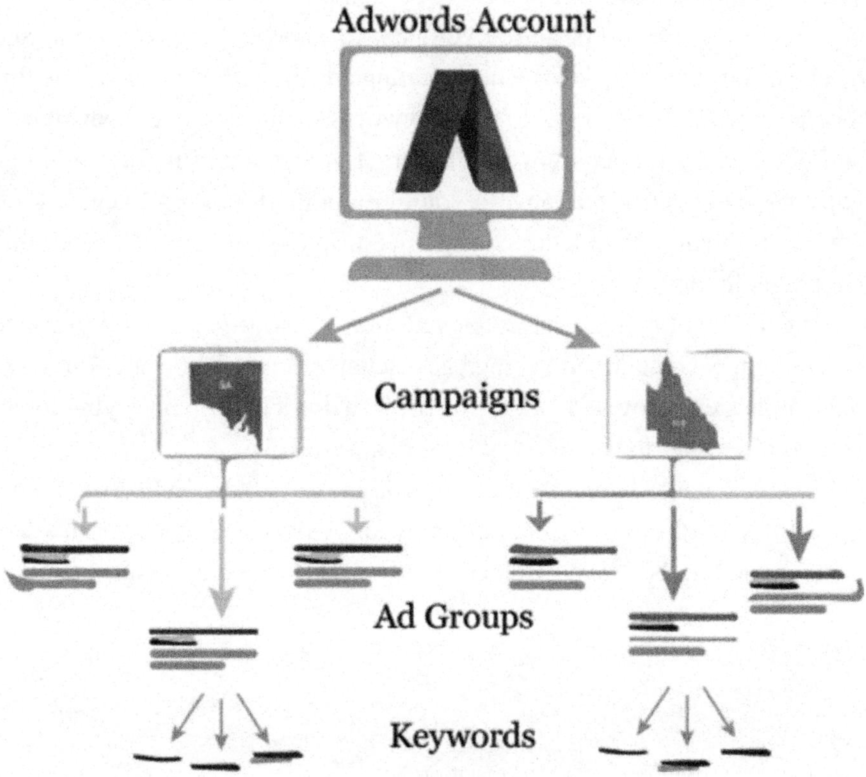

From each campaign you have a series of ad groups, which are the ads that target different areas.

Within each ad group you have your keywords that you aim to target with your ads.

One good way to think about it is that your entire system is based on your selection of keywords—as such, you want to make sure that you have an ideal system. This is where Google AdWords really starts to shine, as they have a specific tool to help you appreciate keywords that you are using, think of new ideas, and optimise for the best possible results.

This tool is often overlooked by AdWords users, so make sure that you get the most out of your experience. You never know where good keywords may lead your business.

Keyword Planner Tool

The Keyword Planner Tool is a free component of Google AdWords designed to guide users and advertisers to choose ideal keywords and discover new keyword ideas when creating ads through AdWords. Use this tool to discover new ways to use keywords, learn about current trends, and develop a stronger campaign to target your niche. The best thing is, with the data readily available to you through the Keyword Planner Tool, keywords are no longer a guessing game; now you can target the ones that people really do use.

The tool is only available to logged in users, so if you are yet to create an account, we recommend going back a chapter in this book and following the simple steps provided—don't worry, you don't need to be paying for an ad to run in order to use the Keyword Planner Tool.

To access the keyword planner tool, you can go to https://adwords.google.com/KeywordPlanner. Or, looking at your AdWords account dashboard, click on the 'Tools' dropdown menu, and select 'Keyword Planner'.

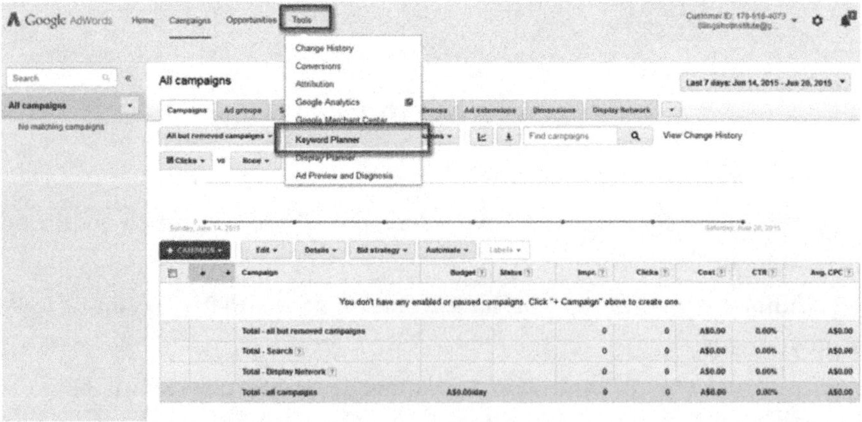

From here you are brought to the start of the Keyword Planner tool; you have a number of options.

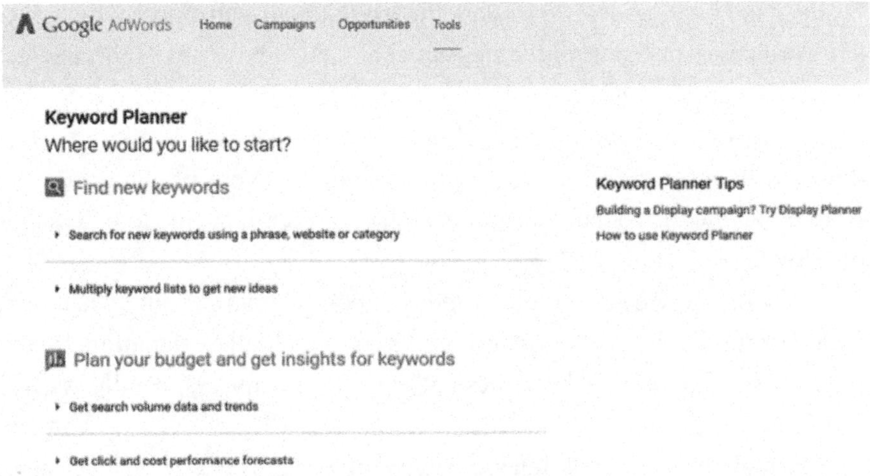

All of these options revolve around keyword data and ideas, and depending on where you are along in the process, each option has its own benefits.

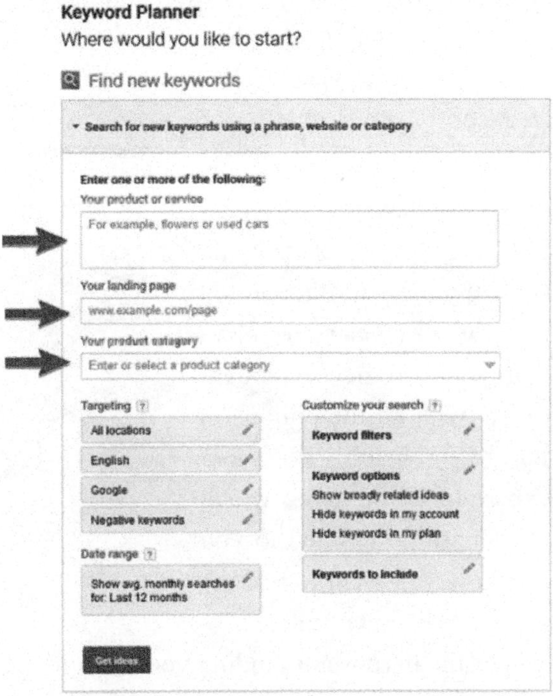

However, it is best to start with the first dropdown areas: 'Search for new keywords using a phrase, website or category'.

This is simply as described: by entering data into either of the three options, you can get keyword ideas and information.

There are a few different benefits to each search type. If you want to know similar keyword ideas to the ones you already have, and want to know how they perform, then try 'Your product or service'.

By searching under 'Your landing page', you can appreciate which keywords your page currently lists under and then try to have that reflected in your advertising efforts.

If you want to take a step back to see which keywords apply to your industry, then select the relevant options from the 'Your product category' drop-down menu. To narrow your searches further, feel free to add data to multiple areas.

You will also see various other options under 'Targeting' and 'Customize your search'. Each of these options comes with a small explanation. So feel free to experiment with how these affect your results, especially when it comes to locations.

The main recommendation here would be to have the relevance selected under keyword options. Simply click on the 'Keyword options'—you should see the first area, 'Only show ideas closely related to my search terms', so switch that to ON.

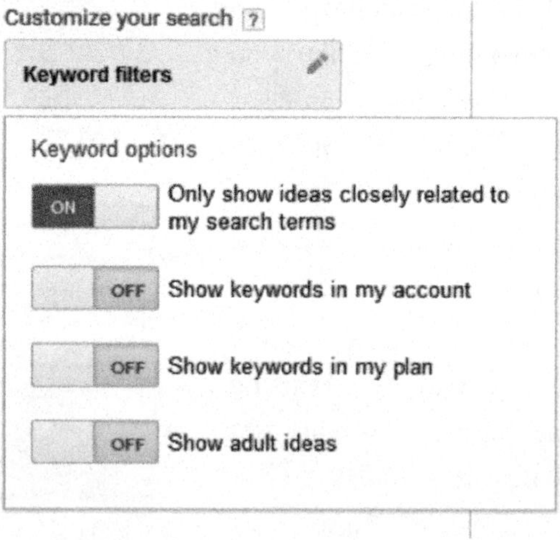

When most people use this tool to search it's important not to be distracted by the more irrelevant keywords searched. On the other hand, by searching with this option off you may get some ideas that you had never thought of. As with all the options in this research tool, it's about experimentation to see which results are best suited to you and how you wish to use the Keyword Planner tool.

For the purpose of guiding you through the tool, let's explore using the word 'flowers'.

The results page that you are met with may seem confusing at first glance, but the information it contains is highly useful to what you are searching for. The first thing you should do is select the ‘Keyword ideas’ tab, rather than the ‘Ad group ideas’ tab. This will narrow it down to individual keywords, rather than grouping them together.

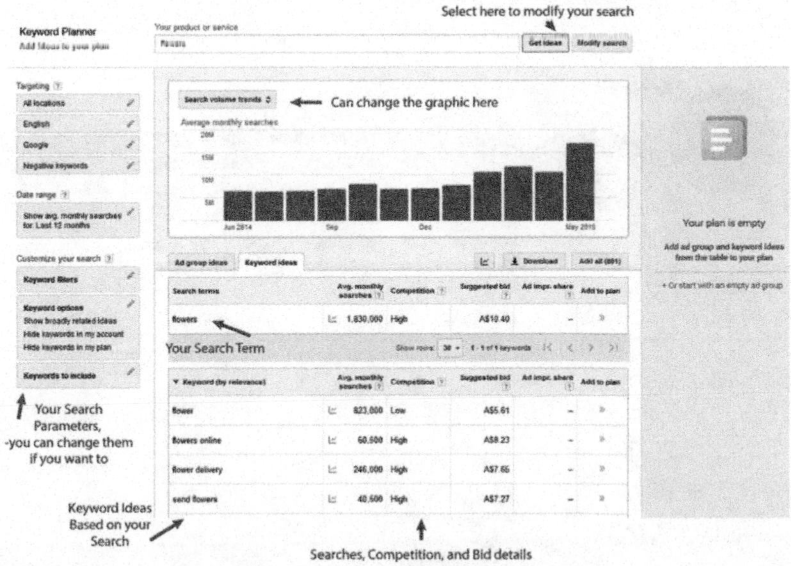

Looking at the results page, you can see a large amount of information.

The term that you searched for will appear in the middle of the page with its relevant statistics. Below this you will find the linking keywords and their details. To the left of the page you can change your search parameters, and in the middle of the page you can see a graph representing the data.

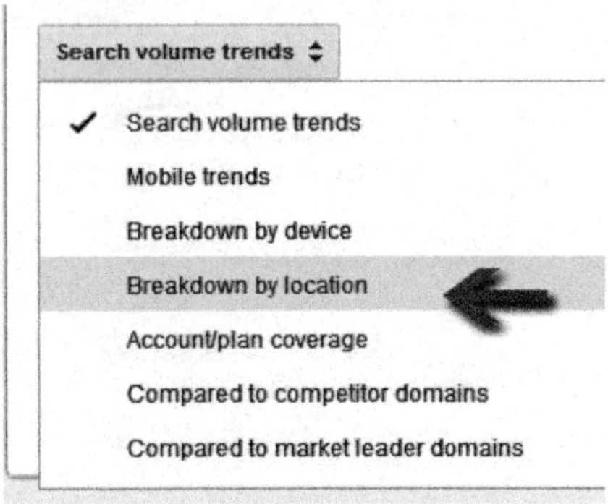

One of the considerations of your search should be your audience and therefore your location. Here, we are looking for flowers, so let's assume that we are a Sydney-based flower business—this means we should be looking for data that is actually relevant to our business. Currently we are searching just for flowers, and we have no locations selected; as such we have over 1.8 million results and we don't know where they come from.

To put it in perspective, change the graphic to display according to location.

Here, for our 'flower' search, we can see that it is actually rather irrelevant to our Sydney-based business, with only 3.4% of the results seen actually coming from Australia.

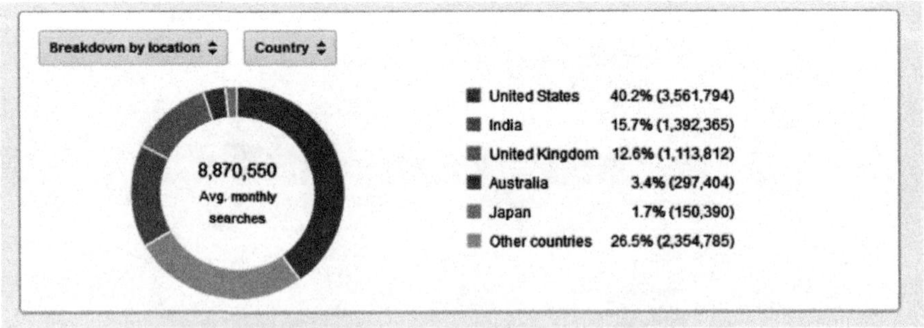

As such, we should change the parameters on the side of the page to add location information, such as 'Australia' or 'Sydney'. Feel free to add multiple cities—this search area is all dependent on the type of business that you are running. For instance, if you are predominantly online and want customers from all over the world, then don't narrow your locations. Alternately, you may be a business that is trying to gain more customers in a specific country, or looking to expand to a new state, and perhaps then you want to see what their specific search statistics are.

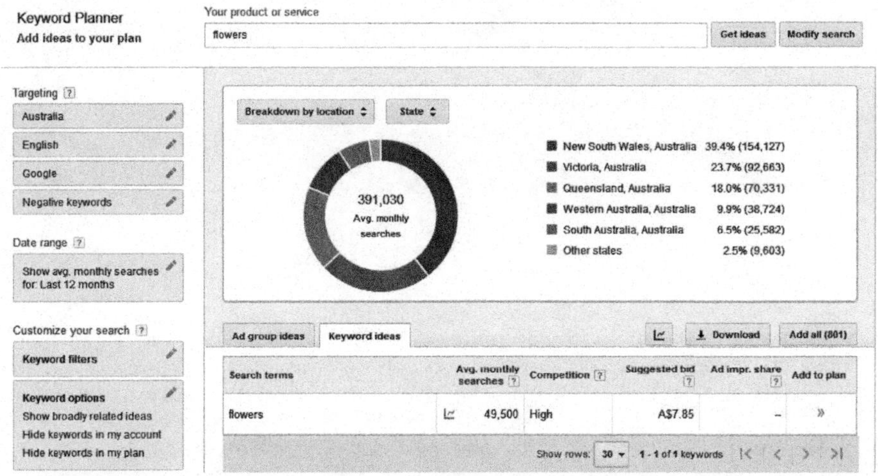

Having now narrowed down our search, we can see a more relevant selection of data. This is what the Keyword Planner tool is all about; balancing the big picture while looking for the most relevant results.

Next, let's have a look through the keywords themselves and determine how to interpret this data. The first step would be to sort the data by 'Avg. monthly searches' so we can appreciate where the highest levels of traffic are. To do this simply click on the relevant box.

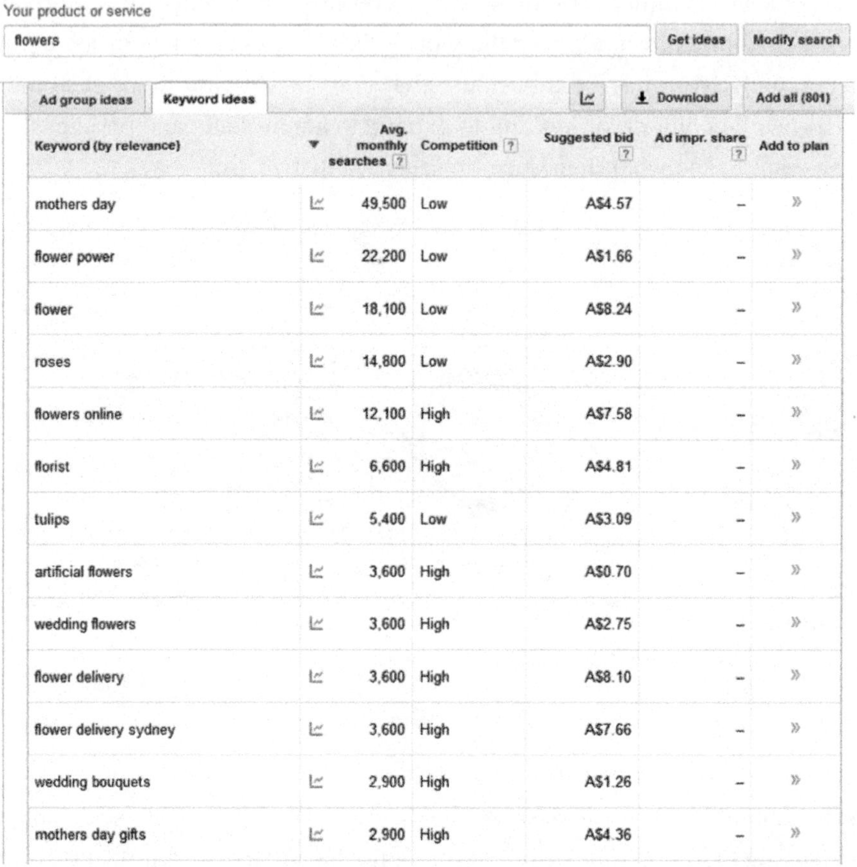
Your product or service

flowers

Get ideas | Modify search

Ad group ideas | Keyword ideas | Download | Add all (801)

Keyword (by relevance)	Avg. monthly searches	Competition	Suggested bid	Ad impr. share	Add to plan
mothers day	49,500	Low	A$4.57	–	»
flower power	22,200	Low	A$1.66	–	»
flower	18,100	Low	A$8.24	–	»
roses	14,800	Low	A$2.90	–	»
flowers online	12,100	High	A$7.58	–	»
florist	6,600	High	A$4.81	–	»
tulips	5,400	Low	A$3.09	–	»
artificial flowers	3,600	High	A$0.70	–	»
wedding flowers	3,600	High	A$2.75	–	»
flower delivery	3,600	High	A$8.10	–	»
flower delivery sydney	3,600	High	A$7.66	–	»
wedding bouquets	2,900	High	A$1.26	–	»
mothers day gifts	2,900	High	A$4.36	–	»

Having sorted our results by average monthly searches, we get a table looking like this.

For a Sydney-based flower business, the result of ‘flower power’ is most likely irrelevant, and the ‘Mother’s Day’ result is seasonal but still a good area to note.

The best way to interpret this data is to compare the elements of searches, competition, and suggested bid.

Search Number

This is an area that is calculated as an average monthly search for the total locations you have selected. The higher the number, the more traffic you can expect to see your ad or to track to your website when ranking well under that keyword.

Competition

This shows what the general level of advertising competition is like for that keyword. The higher the competition, the more popular it is to be targeted. This factor is less important than the other two, but it might just show you the ideal keyword. If a keyword ranks with low competition, then it means investment into this keyword is more likely to pay off than in one with high areas of competition.

Suggested Bid

This area may not seem relevant to you if you don't plan to actually make any bids through AdSense, however it is a great indication to determine just how important the keyword is considered to be. The reason why a bid would be high is because it has a high amount of 'commercial intent'. This means that these are the terms that generally are searched for by customers who are closer to the point of purchasing—often known as 'money keywords'. An example of this difference is a search for terms such as 'Microsoft tablet' versus a search for 'Microsoft Surface 3 new best price'. These keywords tend to be longer and narrower, but they indicate that a searcher knows what they want and is more likely to purchase.

As such, what you want to look for in these three areas is a keyword that has a high number of average monthly searches and a reasonable bid price—if it is low competition then that's even better.

Looking back at our searches, we shall compare a few of the keywords.

Example 1

artificial flowers		3,600	High	A$0.70
wedding flowers		3,600	High	A$2.75
flower delivery		3,600	High	A$8.10

Here, we can see that for each of these results they have the same average searches and the same level of competition, but very different bid suggestions.

The way to interpret this data depends on your intentions as a business. If you are looking for direct business for a popular area, then focus on 'flower delivery'—the high bid suggests that it is a money keyword and is a market with more serious buying interest.

However, if you are not looking to spend as much, then look at 'wedding flowers', as it is still a reasonable bid, but lower than the other, suggesting that a lot of the traffic doesn't always translate into sales, which is what you would expect as a wedding florist.

Example 2

Looking at another set of results:

roses		14,800	Low	A$2.90
flowers online		12,100	High	A$7.58

Here, we can see the comparison between 'roses' and 'flowers online'—they have different results for all three categories and there is an argument for each as the superior choice. 'Roses' receives more traffic and has lower competition. It will be a cheaper campaign, but a lower recommended bid will also suggest less general success. 'Flowers online' has slightly less traffic, and higher competition, but is a larger bid. This indicates that the competition is high because of a high level of interest that equates to direct sales, so if you run a successful campaign you can succeed here—but you may also find limited success due to the competition.

At the end of the day, if you are a florist specialising in roses, then choosing 'roses' as a keyword would be a good choice because it applies to you and you can take advantage of the market while not dedicating too many resources to advertising.

Example 3

mothers day		49,500	Low	A$4.57

As you may recall, the most popular keyword was 'Mother's Day'. Having a large amount of search traffic, a low level of competition, and a reasonable bid, it would make a perfect keyword. However, you need to make sure you are using the Keyword Planner tool to its fullest extent to ensure you don't get trapped by skewed results. This is an obvious example of a keyword that you would only run at certain times of the year—there is no interest in Mother's Day at any time of year except for May or late April.

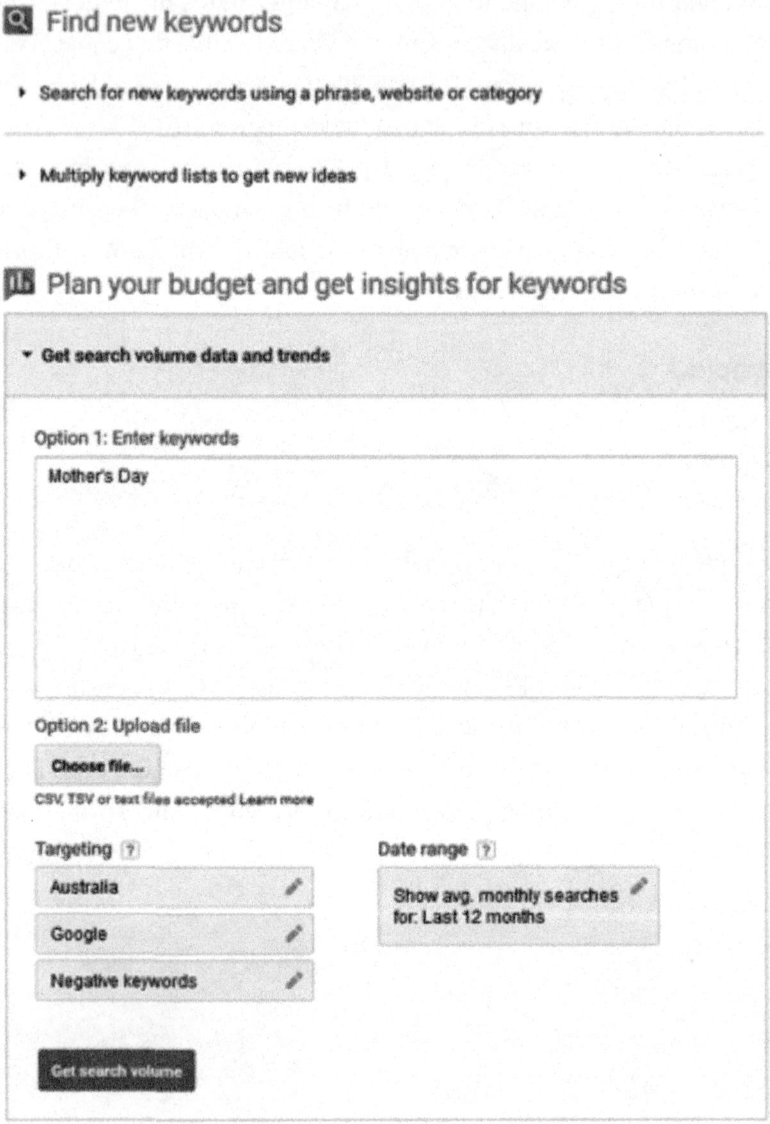

To test this you can run 'Mother's Day' through the Keyword Planner tool.

Start a new search and select 'Get search volume data and trends'. Enter your keyword into the box and run the search to receive more specific data on that keyword (or keywords).

As predicted, the search results show the trends over time.

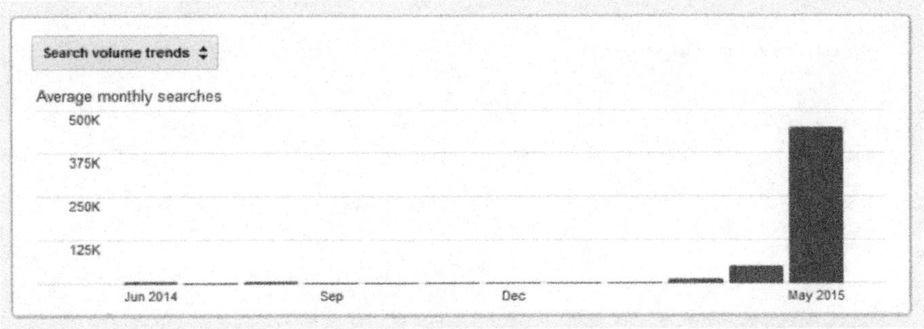

So how can you use this information? Well, if you are the Sydney-based florist that we have been discussing, then you can use this tool to understand which keywords you can use, where the trends are, and which ones to specialise in at certain times of the year. Your AdWords campaign can therefore include a few ads focusing on 'roses', 'flowers online', and 'wedding flowers', plus you can run a specific ad campaign for 'Mother's Day' in April and May.

If still unsure, you can use other elements of the Keyword Planner Tool. A personal favourite for getting perspective on new keywords is the Keyword Multiplier tool.

Finding the Right Keywords

From the first menu on the Keyword Planner tool, select the second option, 'Multiply keyword lists to get new ideas'.

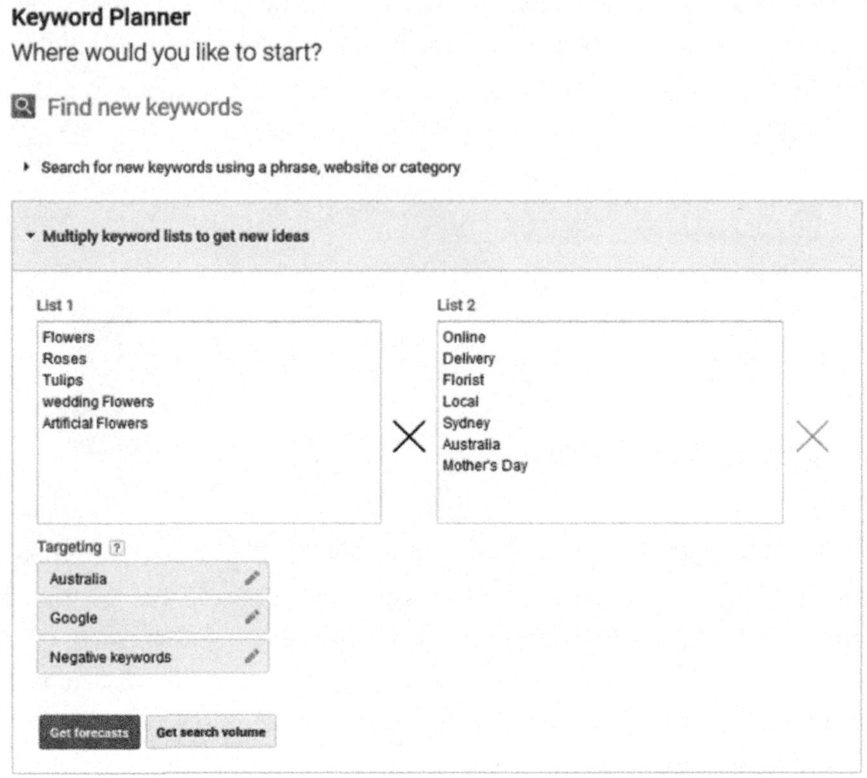

Step 1) Here, we have entered in a number of different keywords and grouped them based on concepts, location, or methods to access them. The idea here is that the two lists will be brought together to create new keywords and we can then see the data for this new information and perhaps get some even better keyword ideas.

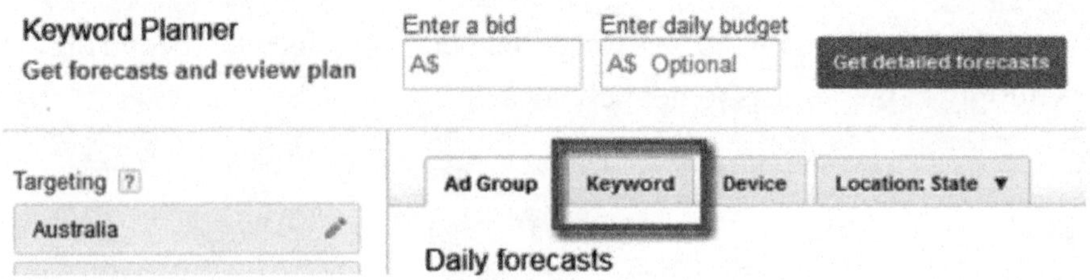

Step 2) Make sure you select the 'keywords' tab to get the desired information.

Step 3) Set a bid.

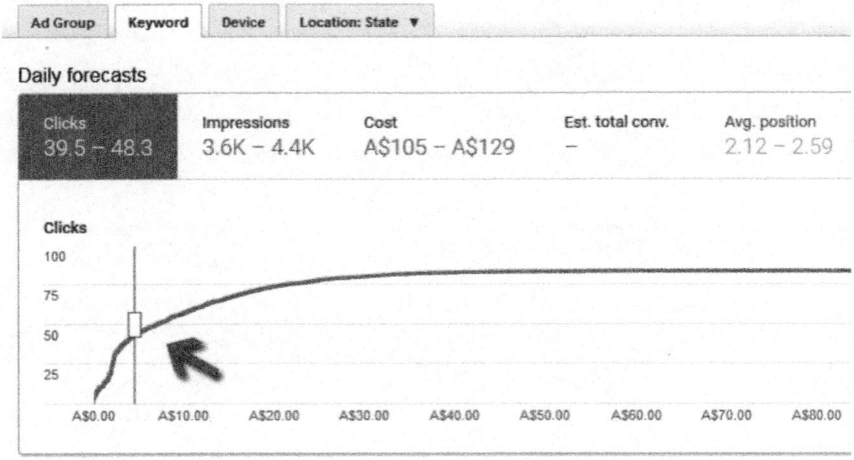

For this part of the tool using 'daily forecasts' you need to set a bid. This allows you to drag the bid slider up or down the slope of the graph to see how your results are most likely to change regarding a balance between investment and number of clicks.

Here, for this graph we can see that there is a point of negligible improvement around the $20–$30 mark where the number of clicks is barely discernible. As such, the wise choice would be to invest $20 for 75 clicks, rather than $80 for 85 clicks.

We have set the bidding slider on the point of the graph with the greatest slope so that we can get a more comprehensive understanding of how it affects our results.

Once you have done this, you can see your results for multiplying keywords.

Step 4) To put it in the most profitable perspective, sort by 'Click'.

Keyword	Ad Group	Max. CPC	Clicks	Impr.	Cost	CTR	Avg. CPC	Avg. Pos.
Flowers Sydney	Flowers Online	A$4.62	12.06	1,036.96	A$33.42	1.2%	A$2.77	2.49
Flowers Australia	Flowers Online	A$4.62	9.48	768.83	A$21.98	1.2%	A$2.32	2.29
Flowers Delivery	Flowers Online	A$4.62	8.06	780.83	A$24.19	1.0%	A$2.99	2.48
Flowers Online	Flowers Online	A$4.62	5.03	749.28	A$11.98	0.7%	A$2.38	2.59
Roses Delivery	Flowers Online	A$4.62	2.42	148.83	A$5.29	1.6%	A$2.19	2.17
wedding Flowers Sydney	Flowers Online	A$4.62	1.42	52.47	A$3.04	2.7%	A$2.14	2.37
Roses Online	Flowers Online	A$4.62	1.42	69.10	A$4.79	2.1%	A$3.37	1.65
Roses Australia	Flowers Online	A$4.62	1.35	136.65	A$4.75	1.0%	A$3.51	1.15
Roses Sydney	Flowers Online	A$4.62	1.09	95.85	A$2.90	1.1%	A$2.64	1.58
wedding Flowers Online	Flowers Online	A$4.62	0.75	42.69	A$2.40	1.7%	A$3.21	1.55
Artificial Flowers Online	Flowers Online	A$4.62	0.53	43.89	A$1.73	1.2%	A$3.25	1.47
Artificial Flowers Sydney	Flowers Online	A$4.62	0.29	25.89	A$0.91	1.1%	A$3.14	1.40
Artificial Flowers Australia	Flowers Online	A$4.62	0.16	5.49	A$0.37	2.0%	A$2.32	1.41
wedding Flowers Australia	Flowers Online	A$4.62	0.11	10.46	A$0.42	1.1%	A$3.67	1.33
Roses Florist	Flowers Online	A$4.62	0.02	9.43	A$0.05	0.2%	A$2.42	1.76
Tulips Online	Flowers Online	A$4.62	0.01	4.63	A$0.00	0.2%	A$0.24	1.63
Flowers Florist	Flowers Online	A$4.62	0.01	3.77	A$0.00	0.2%	A$0.37	2.68
Flowers Local	Flowers Online	A$4.62	0.00	0.00	A$0.00	-	-	-

Step 5) Analyse the results.

Again, this is the challenging part, because it all comes down to the nature of your business. Consider a few different areas of the results board here.

For 'flowers Sydney' the system has predicted the most number of clicks, impressions and cost. We can compare these to a number of the other results, but one of the interesting parts of this feature is to see how various keywords will compare against each other. For instance, looking at the placement of the keywords, the results for 'roses' ranked higher than for 'tulips'. 'Delivery' ranked as being of greater importance than 'online'. And featuring the term 'Sydney' ranked higher than 'Australia'. As such, a focus should be on using 'roses delivery Sydney'.

You can then put this information into a new search to see how it ranks as a keyword. Or you can simply repeat the process with as many factors and details as you wish; the options are up to you and your business needs.

The functions and applications of the Keyword Planner tool are vast—it all comes down to the nature of your business and your imagination for keywords. Depending on how you use the tool there are functions that let you search for specific terms, locations, or applications. You can even multiply lists together to see how a variety of keywords will work together. Ultimately you can see how keywords have performed in the past and how well they might perform in the future. This will all give you new ideas and a new perspective on keywords.

Case Study—Paid Search Tactics Increasing Reach by over 130% in 9 Months

While already dominating the UK market for white goods, consumer electronics, and computing, Dixons Carphone, who owns Currys and PC World, wanted to expand their dominance in the area of online retail cameras.

As with many SEO strategies, it's not just one change that will make the difference—it's numerous tactics working together.

How Currys Achieved the Results They Did

- Conducted a technical audit and from there addressed technical on-page issues on their website in order to improve search rankings and visibility.
- Identifying a gap in the market of DSLR cameras and then focusing a paid search campaign around the top 100 most popular search terms.
- Implementing an outreach campaign to target social media, fans, and industry bloggers—this increased social media numbers and engagement, raised the profile of their blog, and helped them to gain organic links for the DSLR cameras sold on the website.

Results Achieved

Within nine months of implementing and maintaining the SEO and online marketing strategies, Currys achieved the following results:

- 131% increase in reach
- 36% increase in online DSLR camera sales
- 41% increase in revenue
- 300 entries received for the social media photography competition
- 20 keywords moved up to page 1—Currys had ranks 2 and 3 for 'DSLR' and 'DSLR camera' keywords

But what does these all mean in dollar terms? Currys received $480 return for every $1 spent on the paid search campaign.

Chapter 15—Start Your SEO Campaign—Finding the Right Firm

Once you have established that your online business is working using the AdWords test then you can move onto a longer term, more cost effective strategy of using SEO to drive organic traffic to your website. I assume by now you have enough of an idea about SEO to find the right firm to help you achieve your goals. This is a very important step.

If your SEO firm is not talking equally about the 3 Golden Keys I have talked about earlier, then you need to keep looking. Remember, it's not just about one key in isolation. If they are just talking about link-building or only focusing on social media, then you may not be getting the best option.

Here are a few questions to consider asking of your potential firm that may prove very helpful.

How wlll the SEO firm determine which keywords to target?

Research is a critical key to SEO success. If they don't have a research focus your project isn't likely to be successful.

Does your SEO firm have the capacity to do all aspects of web design and coding?

This is becoming more important as the years go by. Once upon a time you could have dedicated SEO firms that knew very little about anything on your website. The firm you choose must have an optimisation program that is capable of and includes an analysis of your site's design, navigation, coding, content, and incoming links. A good SEO firm will be able to provide you with recommendations on improving other areas of your site that either affect search engine placement or the site visitor's experience (graphic design). Site design (layout and graphics) has no bearing on proper search engine optimisation, but site coding, content, and incoming/outgoing links do.

If you have to go back to your graphic designer and then your web designer for every little change that will improve your website's SEO efforts, then it will not only be expensive, but time-consuming too. You want to make sure your site is mobile ready or responsive and that any alterations continue to be integrated into that format. Make sure your website is not entirely built in Flash.

Will they also analyse your competitors' sites and businesses to determine which sites in your industry are performing well and why?

If there is no competitive analysis, then how will they know how to target your competitors? Competitive analysis should be part of your overall business strategy. If your SEO company doesn't understand the difference between your online and offline competitors, then they probably won't understand how to target them either.

Does the SEO firm have content writers in-house?

If the firm does not have someone who specialises in SEO copywriting, look elsewhere. I hope if you are at this part of the book you will understand why this is essential. A good content creation strategy is vital for SEO success. You may be thinking your content is very technical, so a writer cannot write what you know. My answer to that is that you are right; you will have to write the content for much of your site, however it still needs to be written in a way that achieves your SEO goals—using appropriate keywords, for example, is important. This is not so much about good writing but about effective SEO writing, and there is a difference despite Google's assurances that this is not the case.

Does the SEO firm have a link strategy for your site?

This should be a given. If they do not have a link strategy, then they won't be any good. They also need to learn how to employ white hat search techniques and NOT black hat search techniques that could get you banned by Google. Remember, this is not so much about how many links a month they will create, but more about their attitude towards them.

This is a balancing act. There are two extremes you need to be mindful of:

1. They say 'Link-building is dead, we don't do that'
2. They say 'We can build 500 links a month'

In both cases they are not for you—I hope you know why, but let me just remind you. In the first case, they don't want to build links because it's hard work and very time consuming and is probably the biggest cost to an SEO firm's bottom line. They are telling you it's not necessary, hoping you believe that link-building is dead. In the second case, 500 links a month is a very different problem: this still requires lots of work, but the link quality will be very poor and spammy and then you run the risk of getting penalties and being banned on Google. Remember, it's not the volume of links but the quality that takes time and research.

Does the SEO firm handle your social media strategy?

I'm sure you have figured out that a social media strategy is the 3rd Golden Key; all 3 keys need to be managed in the one place for your SEO strategy to fly. Most SEO firms allow you to cherry-pick different plans. For example, you might have them manage the SEO but they don't offer a content plan or a social media plan. My personal feeling is that these days a plan that doesn't incorporate all three keys is misguided and ineffective.

An easy question to ask is if they will post an article or some form of content on social media about once a week. I will tell you why it all needs to be handled as a part of the same strategy: in practical terms, this is how it would work on a weekly basis. The content writer prepares a 200 to 300 word article targeted at a specific keyword as per the overall SEO plan. The web designer and graphic designer make it look good and post it up on the website and/or blog. Then that same article is posted on your various social media networks. Imagine coordinating that every week if it's not all automatically handled by the one firm.

Do they include AdWords/Pay Per Click (PPC) management as a part of their plan?

The PPC plan is a critical part of any SEO strategy so if your SEO firm doesn't see the need to have that sort of data each week and isn't integrating your PPC and organic strategies in a synergistic way, then find someone else. For example, done correctly, the PPC plan should be adjusted over time as your organic SEO traffic kicks in. As your organic traffic captures visitors from certain keywords, then you reduce the PPC keyword reach.

Eventually you will only use your PPC plan for keywords that are impossible to get organically. Otherwise you will be paying for keywords you would have probably captured organically anyway. Remember why you are doing SEO; it's to drive organic traffic to your site so you are not paying for AdWords for the rest of your life.

Is the SEO firm seeking to understand your sales process?

Selling your products or services online is not that radically different to offline. Make sure your prospective firm wants to understand how your products are sold, what questions the customers have, and what objections or concerns they may have. Remember, you know what triggers your prospective customers to buy, but the SEO agency doesn't have a clue. They must drill into this process or you may be barking up the wrong tree.

How do they handle reporting and communication?

Your SEO firm is your marketing partner and there are things you will need from them, like reports. Make sure you find out about the reporting process. Ask for an example of what your reports will look like. You need to know that results are measured and understood. Along with this, ensure you have a contact person in the firm that you can call any time for updates, changes, or even just a bit of advice. Too often I hear of someone that is using a really cheap SEO firm but you can't call them on the phone, all contact is via email; that's a big deal. I'd suggest you be provided at least two ways to contact your account manager—phone, mobile, email, skype. You must to able to communicate with someone on a regular basis who totally understands your strategy and your business. The human element to SEO is the key to its success, not some computer program or algorithm.

Do they offer you quick-fix promises?

Be careful about a firm that promises you it will all happen in the first month. The SEO process is an organic one, which means it's not a quick fix; it will take two to six months to get traction, depending on a bunch of factors. You need to be mindful that this process is not a short term thirty-day process—beware of those that claim otherwise.

Section III Advanced Strategies Online Domination Creating Wealth

Chapter 16—A Local Search Strategy

These advanced strategies are game changers, they are not overly technical, and they may even sound too easy—but they work! This is the most exciting part of this process; this is what will create wealth. These principles are based on traditional business growth models, just replicated online.

Google Search is becoming more and more local as the years roll on. In other words, if you Google 'Greek restaurant' on your phone or computer in your house you will notice that Google will list the Greek restaurants nearby in your search results. Then if you call your friend in another state and ask them to do that same search, they will get an entire page of different results. This miracle is called 'local search'. Google understands that if you want to eat Greek food you probably don't really need to know which Greek restaurants are 1000 miles away; you will starve to death getting there. For Google to be the best search engine, it needs to be accurate, relevant, and localised.

What I'm talking about here is Google Local Search and how it is changing the way we shop and make purchase decisions. Consider these three new realities as discussed by Samerr Samat, VP Product Management at Google:

> Foot traffic has always mattered most to local retailers, but the way it's achieved is changing fast. On-the-go consumers now spend more than 15 hours per week researching on their smartphones. They gather information and 'snack shop' at the pace and place that suits them best—not just on their smartphone, but at the office desktop and at home on the couch with a tablet.
>
> This change in consumer behavior is creating dramatic new realities in the world of local retail. It's not only changing the mind-set of consumers

as they walk into the store, but it's also changing actual foot traffic patterns. Holiday store visits dropped 55% from 38 billion in 2010 to 17 billion in 2013, according to Shoppertrak. Yet during that same period, same store sales rose, according to MasterCard's SpendPulse report, which means that the value of each store visit actually doubled. How? Consumers visited less, but they were better informed about what they wanted when entering the store. Each trip was more purposeful and they bought more.

Our new Digital Impact On In-Store Shopping study, commissioned from Ipsos MediaCT and Sterling Brands, shows just how digital now creates foot traffic by leading shoppers to stores, then helps convert them once they're in-store. The research illustrates why it's so important for retailers to think of blending their digital presence with their physical stores. Brands such as Macy's, REI and Sephora are leading the way on this front. They're offering in-store pickup for items bought online, supporting home delivery of products purchased in-store and showing product availability at nearby stores in search results. These strategies not only create a better experience for shoppers, but they also boost the bottom line.

In short, both research and retail trends show that the way to reach today's shoppers is to care less about where a sale happens and more about how to make it happen in the way the consumer wants at that moment. So let's take a look at the three new realities of local retail driven by these changes in consumer behavior. We'll review the research and see how some fearless retail leaders have already bridged the online-offline divide to create a profitable omnichannel connection.

New reality #1: Digital drives in-store traffic

As it turns out, digital doesn't just drive e-commerce. It actually gets consumers into local stores. A 2014 study on local search behavior found that 50% of consumers will visit a store within one day of a local search on their smartphone. Scott Zalaznik, Sprint's vice president of digital, has seen digital's influence on offline shopping firsthand: "Ninety percent of our customers start their journey online but buy in-store."

For some shoppers, the local store is still a place to browse and talk to experts, but for others, it's becoming more like a local distribution center where they can pop in quickly to pick up a product they've researched in advance. When asked what information would be helpful to have in local search results, respondents in our Digital Impact on In-Store Shopping study listed "product availability at a nearby store" (74%) and "pricing at that store" (75%). That's why it's important to promote and share inventory seamlessly across all channels.

Bridget Dolan, vice president of interactive marketing at Sephora, agrees that online activity affects offline behavior, especially with regard to smartphones. As she puts it, "In retail, you can't think about the mobile phone as a threat. You have to think about it as a magnet that draws people into your stores."

Macy's vice president of marketing strategy, Serena Potter, says the retail giant makes sure that its local store inventory is visible to anyone browsing its website or Google Search. The brand uses Google Local Inventory Ads to connect shoppers with information about the products they seek. "We can tell her that there are eight of what she wants in her size and desired color available right now in the store that's five blocks away."

New reality #2: Smartphones are in-store shopping assistants

Thanks to our constantly connected world, we've become accustomed to instantaneous answers and a wealth of information at our fingertips, but not all retailers have translated this well into in-store experiences. Shoppers are increasingly frustrated by the lack of in-store information. Two-thirds of those surveyed said they couldn't find the details they needed while visiting a store. Many, as a result, are turning to their smartphone to fill in the information gap. Of the 42% who research online while in stores, almost half use the retailer's own site or app. And one in three shoppers actually prefer to use their smartphone to find additional information rather than ask a store employee for help, according to our Mobile In-Store Research study.

Annie Zipfel, senior vice president of marketing for outdoor retailer REI, says, "The consumer has never been more informed, and that information comes from their phone. We love when someone enters the store holding their phone saying, 'I want this tent. I want this bike. Help me find this.'" It's a perfect example of how digital and local retail can come together to make the sale.

Even if shoppers want to showroom, or browse in-store with the intent to buy online later, they're likely turning to their phone in those moments. So make sure your mobile presence is working on your behalf. Contrary to popular sentiment, Best Buy CEO Hubert Joly actually says, "We love being used as the internet's showroom." He thinks that once customers are in your store, they're yours to lose. The key is to give them all the online information they need at their fingertips via your site, app and search campaigns to enable them to make a decision and buy in your store.

New reality #3: Omnichannel shopping calls for omnichannel measurement

Though shopping habits have changed drastically, retailers haven't necessarily caught up in the ways they measure their marketing efforts and allocate their media spend. Most retailers don't yet understand the extent to which digital drives in-store transactions and how in-store visits affect online purchases. The result is that they're often viewing sales in silos and undervaluing the real impact of their digital spend on total sales. Consequently, they're making suboptimal decisions about their media mix.

Macys.com's Serena Potter says the brand has placed a special focus on understanding just how much of local business sales come from digital searches. "We've been able to show that for every dollar we invest in search, we drive $6 of sales in-store," she says. Smart marketers such as Jennifer Kasper, group vice president of digital media and multi-cultural marketing for Macy's, are doing their best to break down traditional measurement silos and look at what drives sales in a more holistic way. They're no longer treating digital and in-store sales as separate teams with different objectives; rather, they're combining them and aligning on company-wide goals, such as overall sales, to pursue collectively. "The bottom line is we're indifferent to whether a shopper converts in the store or online; we just want her to shop with Macy's," Kasper explains. The future of shopping.

The bridge between digital traffic and foot traffic has become a competitive necessity in retail. The retailers who embrace these new realities—who connect with their customers seamlessly, no matter where those shoppers happen to be or how they want to buy—will be the retailers who win. It's those on-the-go connections that are the future of shopping.

https://www.thinkwithgoogle.com/articles/3-new-realities-of-local-retail.html

So you may be asking, how do I ensure that my website is benefitting from this trend towards local search? First of all, it might just be easier to explain it this way. One of the ways Google achieves this local search objective is called Google Places. Google establishes where you physically are by inviting a business or website owner to register their location in Google Places. Simply search for the term 'Google places for business' and just follow the instructions to fill in the relevant information address details, then Google will kindly post you a letter using snail mail to that address with a PIN code. This is to confirm you are actually at that location and are not just making it up. Once you get your mail, you verify your location listing by typing in the PIN code, then Google will accept your listing as legitimate.

You may now be thinking about how you can make money from this when you are physically only in one location. In the old days if you wanted to expand your business into new markets, you would go and open a new branch office or a franchise or store in a different city and hope for the best. This is what very large organisations have done for over a hundred years and it works very well, especially in the physical goods and services business. As an example, McDonalds needs to be close by or you won't be eating it—plain and simple.

In the new digital world, the landscape is very different. If your online business can serve the entire city or state or country then you don't have to open a network of branch offices to be successful. However, depending on your product or service you may not get any ranking in Google outside of your local area where you are physically located. This is a problem if you live in a two-horse town or believe your product needs to reach a bigger market.

For example, one of the online businesses I run is a service that people want to source locally but in reality it can be provided from anywhere in the country. For whatever reason for some products and services your customers may feel more comfortable buying the product from someone in the same city, although they never walk into the office or store or physically meet anyone; it's a part of how we are wired as humans. I knew my website was doing well in my local area and I also know I am in a very small market geographically. I live in a city of about 800,000 people and my potential market across just two larger cities was five million people.

It didn't take me too long to solve the problem and you have probably already figured out where this is heading, but I will walk you through it anyway. All I needed to do was open two more offices in those cities.

However, if you remember some of my rules earlier, I don't do staff and I don't do financial commitments like commercial office leases. There is another option custom-built for this exact problem. It's called a serviced office or shared office. In almost every city there are firms that charge a nominal amount of money, typically between $80 and $200 per month, for you to have a virtual address/office. What this means is that you can use the address (it's normally a prime CBD location) with an actual office, with a receptionist and all the office trimmings. If, for whatever reason, you need to use the office, it has board rooms you can book, etc. But what this does, most importantly, is allows you to receive mail to that location (Google doesn't do postal office or postal boxes). So once you have signed up for this location you can then have Google post you a letter, and bingo! You are in business in that location for a fraction of the cost of everyone else in that city.

By the way, there is one more thing you had better take care of to have this strategy fly. Change your phone number from the local number to a 1300 or 1800, otherwise your potential customers will get very confused. If a prospective client asks during that initial phone call where you are physically located while they are talking to you, they ask this because you have a national phone number—these days when you call the 1300 or 1800 numbers you get a large call centre overseas so people are a bit wary of them; you must always be truthful. Don't try to trick anyone here, simply tell them where you are but that you have an office in (tell them the street name, it will be well known because they are locals). Generally at that point no one cares—they just need you to help them.

Most websites go to great lengths to avoid this problem by not posting any address or phone number on them. How many times have you spent a ridiculous amount of time trying to find a phone number on a website? It would be hilarious if it wasn't so important.

As you can imagine, once my market increased from 800,000 people to 5.8 million people, my sales went through the roof, and all for an additional $260 per month in my particular case. My suggestion is that before you go and organise 200 virtual offices around the country, start with one location first so you can test if this strategy will work for you.

Chapter 17—The Monopoly Mindset

Everyone loves playing Monopoly. The key to winning Monopoly is to buy as much property as possible or at least more than anyone else in the game. I remember as a kid, if you could own one whole side of the board and put motels on it then you were well on your way to winning the game. The excitement of someone working their way along that side of the board as they rolled the dice was amazing.

Generally speaking, in the business world the word 'monopoly' is full of negative and sinister connotations, but for the entrepreneur, it's not negative but more a mindset and a way of thinking. This next strategy requires that sort of thinking. Once you have a website making you money and you know that the numbers are working, you begin to create a monopoly. Here is a tip for you; if you don't already know, rich people love monopolies and poor people think they're unethical. Bill Gates loves buying smaller companies that could potentially compete in the software market. Rupert Murdoch made a point of buying all the local newspapers around the country to prevent opposition. Then, to make things more difficult for someone to get into the newspaper game, he would pay companies to dismantle and destroy the printing presses once they were getting old or outdated to make sure no one else could start competing in that market. The rich have been carefully controlling their particular markets for thousands of years. You have two choices; get bitter about it, or join them.

Once you have a website that is making you money and you want to get more market share, build another website. This is not a very complex strategy. You need to know what you are doing here; Google doesn't really want you to be doing it of course. What Google wants is for each business to have one website, so that when you go onto Google to buy car insurance you can look at the ten different company offerings on the first page of

Google to get the best choice. This is Google's objective and I'm sure in years to come they may achieve this objective, but for now, in 2016, it's open slather as long as you follow some very commonsense rules.

Discuss this strategy with your SEO firm and if they don't think it's a good idea then find another firm. Let's put it this way: there are six listings on the first page of Google that really get almost all the traffic. The first three are AdWords (this can vary depending on the search) and then you have the top three organic listings. With one website ranking in the top three of Google and one AdWords campaign, you potentially may get about 20% of all the traffic from that page. With a total of three websites ranking in the top three spots organically and three AdWords campaigns, that number increases to about 85% of the traffic from that page. Now ask yourself: with that sort of increase in traffic, can you afford to build a few more websites and run AdWords campaigns? If you are really of the monopoly mindset, then build a few more websites and dominate the entire first page of Google. Remember, these days the battle for online supremacy is fought out on page one of Google. If you are on page two or three you may as well have not built the website. Just a few words of warning about this strategy: the copywriting or content on each of these additional sites must be different and pass the Copyscape test or it will get penalised by Google. Secondly, make the site look different; your customers don't want to see a replica of the last site they visited or they will just bounce out of it quickly, which will really hurt your SEO efforts. I would suggest the second and third sites have a different approach and target a different potential client, or if your message is exactly the same, use a different website template, logo, colours, and images.

Chapter 18—Free Offering Strategy—A Matter of Trust

Everyone loves something for free. If you want to build a wonderful list of prospective customers or simply just make more sales, provide your visitors with amazing freebies. A good example of this is Apple's iTunes product: it's free for anyone who has a computer, and it allows you to manage your music, podcasts, videos, etc. in a wonderful way. If you have an iPod or an iPhone, it will interface nicely with your computer. iTunes is free, there is no obligation with downloading it, you are not forced into buying anything; it's just free. Naturally, if you want to buy music or movies using this free platform, you can and people do. iTunes is a multibillion-dollar product; an entire industry, in fact. To cite another example, Facebook is also free and so is Google. Both of these companies make billions of dollars, but at their heart they give amazing value to customers for free.

How you view your free offering is critical to building wealth. Your free offering provides an initial step or platform to work from in the buying cycle. In other words, see your first free offering to your clients as the most important step, because once they access the free offering they become, in effect, your customer; they just haven't spent any money yet. They are buying into your brand. They are taking that critical first step in building a relationship with you.

What is important is that you have more to offer your customers beyond that first freebie, otherwise you will go broke pretty quickly. You want to create an entire suite of products, starting small and working up to the larger, more expensive products. McDonalds built its business on $1 burgers. Now if you walk into McDonalds it's about a $10 minimum spend for a meal deal. No one thinks about the $1 burger anymore, just a meal deal. This reveals a wonderful marketing strategy that applies to any and all online businesses.

You may be wondering what you could do or give away for free as part of your online strategy. It could be an e-book, a white paper, a consultation, a video, a report, an evaluation, a podcast, a newsletter; the list is endless. Just make sure that your free offering is on your home page or landing page and that all your visitors need to do is give you their name, email address, and/or phone number. This will help you to build your list of prospects and, more importantly, engage your potential customers in the buying relationship by carrying out a transaction. If your offering is good and not rubbish, then they will trust you with another transaction because the first one was a pleasant experience. Remember that people buy from people they trust—even if your market is B2B it's still people buying from people. If their first experience is good then the trust levels go through the roof.

Be generous and don't approach this free offering with a stingy mindset because your customers will feel it and your opportunity to build trust with them will be lost. Think about your own experiences whenever some company or website has given you a freebie that exceeds your expectations. You automatically trust them with what they will give you if you buy their product or service. Think about when you have felt like the freebie was so crap that it killed the trust you had to make another transaction with them. How many times have you reluctantly come across one of these types of sites where if you want the information, you need to give out your details. This strategy is ok by the way, but not if when you finally get the freebie that you reluctantly signed up for its complete rubbish—the eBook is four pages of nothing, you glance at it for three seconds, and delete it off your computer. You feel tricked and as result you don't ever buy anything from them because you have no choice but to assume that you will be tricked again.

I remember when my wife and I first got married we saved up for about a year, and instead of buying a house like most normal couples our age, we decided to take our money we had saved and take a one-year world trip. As a new husband I decided to surprise my new bride with this plan so I went and spent about $10,000 and bought the tickets, came home, and announced it to my very kind and patient wife. (Did I mention I had only been married about six months at the time? I was new to the marriage business.) I was very excited and my wife was luckily happy also. Looking back now, she probably thought she'd married a total idiot, and buying a house would have been a far more sensible option. I assured her however that we had the rest of our lives to have a mortgage and kids, and this option wouldn't be viable again until we were old and retired. It was the best pitch I ever gave and so off we went.

Leaving the shores of Australia for twelve months was amazing. The first place we visited was Hawaii, a wonderful place full of interesting things to see and nice beaches—not quite Australian beaches, but still ok. My wife and I were in a shopping centre looking around, with our backpacks on and matching tracksuits, when a guy with a beautiful parrot on his shoulder approached us and asked if we would like to put his parrot on our shoulders so we could take a photo of it. We both were very happy to so we gave him our camera and he carefully put the bird on my wife's shoulder and he kindly took a photo for us. He then handed us back the camera and took back the bird. We thanked him very much for his kindness and then to our horror he said, "That will be $10." For whatever reason we were naive to the ways of slick marketing at the time so we felt manipulated and deceived. I told him he wasn't getting a penny and if he had told us upfront he wanted $10 for the trouble we would have politely declined his offer. He was very unimpressed and told us what he thought of us and I retorted accordingly. As I look back now, it was not really that big of a deal. If we had been American he wouldn't have had to ask for money—we would have probably just given the guy a tip and all would have been well. But Australians don't tip; the only tip you will get from an Australian is which horse to bet on and that's about it.

The reason I share that story with you is that if you leave your customers feeling deceived or tricked with your free offering you have wasted the opportunity and potentially lost a lifetime customer.

Chapter 19—Become an Expert by Publishing

You may feel you don't know enough to be an expert in your respective field, but most of the knowledge you have would be of great value to someone else, somewhere. I don't care whether your field of expertise is hamsters or hamstrings; your knowledge, which ultimately becomes your intellectual property, can be of great value to someone else. Don't think you need to be a world leading expert in your field before you can help others out online with what you know. In fact, there will always be someone else who knows far more about any given subject than you, but here's a newsflash: they will probably never be your customer because they already know what you know, but the other 99.9% of the world's population could benefit from what you know.

There is an old maxim used in the academic world that goes something like this: 'publish or perish'. In other words, if you want a career as a successful academic, you need to publish; this sets up the academic as a published expert and makes the university look good too. It's not that radically different in the business world. You set yourself up as an expert and it makes whatever your online business is look good as well.

Your subject or content doesn't have to be unique or magically creative. Don't worry yourself with the objection of whether or not someone in your niche has already published something similar. When you go to a bookstore there will often be ten books published on the exact same subject, sometimes more—however each book is unique in its own way, bringing a unique offering to the market.

There are many things you can do to start in this endeavour, but the best advice I could give you is to write a book. I know it sounds crazy but it serves another very important purpose other than the ones mentioned above already. It acts as a foundation for content for your website, blog, and social media campaigns for years to come. Each week or month or whenever you like, you may want to post some new content on your website. A book that you have taken time to write will have potentially hundreds of mini subjects that you can re-purpose for your website. I'm not suggesting you just publish an entire chapter each week and that's that. Be a little creative here; you may want to attach a graphic or introduce the topic in a different way.

As a busy business owner one of the most important things you can do is produce intellectual property; it will make you money. One of the obvious challenges is a lack of time and coming up with a new idea for content each week can be difficult. A book of about 40,000 words will provide your audience with plenty to chew on each week or whenever you post to your website.

Another one of your objections may well be that you can't write a coherent sentence to save your life. This may well be true. There are a range of options here, but a simple solution is to find a freelance writer to help you put your book together, either as a collaborative effort or as a ghostwriter. Either way it will help you to polish your message.

Chapter 20—Finding the Right Business Idea

What problem are you solving? This is an easy thing to think of when considering what kind of online business you may want to get into, or a wonderful focus if you already have a business up and running. People will pay money to have their problems solved. Whether it's helping them find the nearest shoe store or the best solar panel on the market, if you can focus on the problem you are solving and do it well, then you are on your way to creating a wonderful online business.

Don't get too worked up if your idea isn't unique or is already out in the marketplace. It's not really about the idea as much as it is about the execution of the idea, or in other words, how well you deliver your product or service to the market. A simple example is the way Apple operates. In case you didn't know they didn't invent the portable MP3 player, or the iPad; both concepts were already out in the marketplace years before Apple went to market with both of these products. What they did exceptionally well was execute a brilliant marketing campaign to make their re-imagined, already in the marketplace product better than anyone else's. If you had an MP3 player, pre-iPod nobody cared, but if you had one of those little white boxes with an apple on it, you were cool.

Don't be afraid because you are not a world expert on the niche you are marketing to. If you think about it, in most cases the marketing and customer experience matter far more than your product knowledge or experience in your niche.

You already have enough ideas and experience to make a few ideas fly. Whether it's your profession, hobby, or just a passing interest, you can create an online business from it. There are plenty of ordinary people around who have made millions from a simple idea that was of interest to them, often starting from very unremarkable circumstances. Mark Zuckerberg, the Facebook founder, just thought his idea would be fun for the students at his university. Brainstorm some things you're passionate about and develop them into an online business.

You may have experienced some frustration in your own life with a website, product, or service when you said to yourself, "I could do this better than these guys." This is another way to start thinking about the experiences you have in your own life that can be the inspiration for an online business.

Chapter 21—SEO Toolbox and Freebies

These cool tools are also found throughout the relevant chapters but are here as an easy reference. Just a note here: some of these tools are very similar and in many cases it just comes down to personal preference.

Thanks Amy, I notice we are not on page 15 of Google anymore we have moved up to page 3, that's good right?

Pay-Per-Click Marketing

- Bruce Clay PPC tutorial—outlines PPC basics and provides suggestions
- http://www.bruceclay.com/ppc/pay-per-click.htm
- Google Keyword Planner—PPC keyword research tool

- https://adwords.google.com/ko/KeywordPlanner/Home
- Wordstream—PPC marketing tools and blog
- http://www.wordstream.com/pay-per-click
- Wordstream's guide to choosing a PPC platform
- http://marketing.wordstream.com/How-To-Choose-A-PPC-Software-Platform-Buying-Guide.html
- UnBounce—landing page creator
- www.unbounce.com

Tools from Google

Google offers a number of tools that should be in every SEO toolkit:

- Google Analytics http://www.google.com/analytics/
- Google Keyword Planner Tool
- https://adwords.google.com/ko/KeywordPlanner/Home
- Google Webmaster Tools https://www.google.com/webmasters/tools/home?hl=en

Local Marketing

- Local SEO guide http://www.localseoguide.com/
- Local SEO tools http://www.localseoguide.com/local-seo-tools/
- Optimising for local search http://www.quicksprout.com/2012/03/26/how-to-optimize-your-business-for-local-search-and-social-marketing/
- Local search tips
- http://blog.crazyegg.com/2013/05/16/local-search-optimization-tips/

Content Marketing and Copywriting Tools and Resources

- Addvocate—content sharing platform for companies https://addvocate.com/
- Convert—A/B testing for more effective content http://www.convert.com/
- Copyblogger—tools and resources for content marketers
- http://www.copyblogger.com/
- Curata—content creation software http://www.curata.com/
- Inbound Writer—content performance and analytics software
- http://www.inboundwriter.com/
- Optimizely—A/B testing for more effective content https://www.optimizely.com/
- Outbrain—content curation http://www.outbrain.com/select
- Papershare—content generation platform http://www.papershare.com/
- Parse.ly—predicts content performance with audience http://www.parsely.com/
- Percolate—content marketing platform http://percolate.com/
- ProBlogger—building a better blog http://www.problogger.net/
- Scribe—content marketing software by CopyBlogger http://scribecontent.com/
- SEOBook—optimising your blog http://www.seobook.com
- UberFlip—content hub creation http://www.uberflip.com/

Social Media Marketing Tools and Resources

- Hootsuite—content management, engagement tracking, scheduling platform
- http://www.hootsuite.com/

- Jon Loomer—advanced Facebook marketing blog http://www.jonloomer.com/
- Mention—social sentiment/brand, name mentions tracker https://en.mention.com/
- RazorSocial—social media marketing blog http://www.razorsocial.com/blog/
- Social Media Examiner—tips for using social media for business
- http://www.socialmediaexaminer.com
- Social Media Marketing Magazine—industry publication for social media marketers
- http://www.smmmagazine.com/
- Social Mention—sentiment tracking, analytics http://www.socialmention.com /
- SocialMouths—social media marketing blog http://socialmouths.com/blog/
- SocialOomph—fully integrated platform, allows you to schedule content across networks, track mentions, engage with followers, etc. https://www.socialoomph.com/
- Twazzup—Twitter monitoring http://www.twazzup.com/
- Tweetdeck—engage with Twitter followers in real-time, track mentions and engagement https://tweetdeck.twitter.com/

Link-Building Tools

- Ahrefs—backlink checker and analysis tool https://ahrefs.com/
- BuzzStream—link research and link-building tool http://www.buzzstream.com/
- GSA Search Engine Ranker—niche backlink-building tool
- https://secure.avangate.com/order/product.php?PRODS=4555684&QTY=1&AFFILIATE=48198
- Inspyder Backlink Monitor—backlink analysis tool

- http://www.inspyder.com/products/BacklinkMonitor/Default.aspx
- Link Emperor—tool used to build authority links
- http://www.linkemperor.com/?a=ec6ce75b4ecf
- Link prospector—helps users build targeted backlinks
- http://linkprospector.citationlabs.com/
- Majestic SEO—backlink checker and site exploration tool
- http://www.majesticseo.com/
- Open Site Explorer—discover new linking opportunities
- http://www.opensiteexplorer.org/
- Rankwyz—link-building tool http://www.rankwyz.com/
- ScrapeBox—pinging, commenting, link-building tool http://www.scrapebox.com/

Charles's Insight

There is nothing like discovering all these cool tools that essentially let you know how much work still needs to be done. Generally, if you are anything like me, the thought of paying someone to do something that you could possibly do if you just had an extra five hours a day is terrifying. But once you have run your site through a few of these tools you will soon realise that much of this is well beyond the DIY ability.

If you want to make money from your website, focus on your product or service; leave the SEO nightmare to someone who knows what they are doing.

Things are changing so rapidly in this space that the average small business owner has no hope of keeping up. Focus on making money and building wealth. The best way I can explain it is this: you know that keeping an eye on your money in your business is critical, right? Making sure you do your taxes properly is also critical. But this doesn't mean you have to understand all the ins and outs of taxation law to run a business; you just find the right bean counter to help you. So it goes with online marketing; your success or failure could simply be your attitude. I love the DIY mentality of the small business owner, but in the case of SEO—OUTSOURCE!

Printed in Dunstable, United Kingdom

91218903R00107